ASVAB Math Tutor

Everything You Need to Help Achieve an Excellent Score

By

Reza Nazari

&

Ava Ross

All inquiries should be addressed to:

info@effortlessMath.com

www.EffortlessMath.com

All inquiries should be addressed to:

info@effortlessMath.com

www.EffortlessMath.com

ISBN: 978-1-64612-844-0

Published by: **Effortless Math Education Inc.**

for Online Math Practice Visit **www.EffortlessMath.com**

Welcome to

ASVAB Math Prep
2021

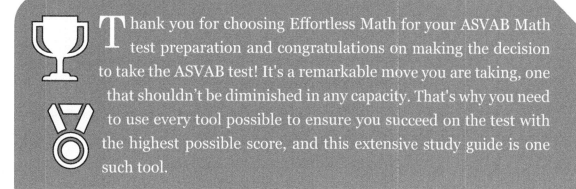

Thank you for choosing Effortless Math for your ASVAB Math test preparation and congratulations on making the decision to take the ASVAB test! It's a remarkable move you are taking, one that shouldn't be diminished in any capacity. That's why you need to use every tool possible to ensure you succeed on the test with the highest possible score, and this extensive study guide is one such tool.

If math has never been a strong subject for you, **don't worry**! This book will help you prepare for (and even ACE) the ASVAB test's math section. As test day draws nearer, effective preparation becomes increasingly more important. Thankfully, you have this comprehensive study guide to help you get ready for the test. With this guide, you can feel confident that you will be more than ready for the ASVAB Math test when the time comes.

First and foremost, it is important to note that this book is a study guide and not a textbook. It is best read from cover to cover. Every lesson of this "self-guided math book" was carefully developed to ensure that you are making the most effective use of your time while preparing for the test. This up-to-date guide reflects the 2021 test guidelines and will put you on the right track to hone your math skills, overcome exam anxiety, and boost your confidence, so that you can have your best to succeed on the ASVAB Math test.

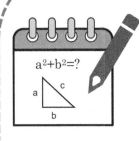

This study guide will:

☑ Explain the format of the ASVAB Math test.

☑ Describe specific test-taking strategies that you can use on the test.

☑ Provide ASVAB Math test-taking tips.

☑ Review all ASVAB Math concepts and topics you will be tested on.

☑ Help you identify the areas in which you need to concentrate your study time.

☑ Offer exercises that help you develop the basic math skills you will learn in each section.

☑ Give **2 realistic and full-length practice tests** (featuring new question types) with detailed answers to help you measure your exam readiness and build confidence.

This resource contains everything you will ever need to succeed on the ASVAB Math test. You'll get in-depth instructions on every math topic as well as tips and techniques on how to answer each question type. You'll also get plenty of practice questions to boost your test-taking confidence.

In addition, in the following pages you'll find:

➢ **How to Use This Book Effectively** – This section provides you with step-by-step instructions on how to get the most out of this comprehensive study guide.

➢ **How to study for the ASVAB Math Test** – A six-step study program has been developed to help you make the best use of this book and prepare for your ASVAB Math test. Here you'll find tips and strategies to guide your study program and help you understand ASVAB Math and how to ace the test.

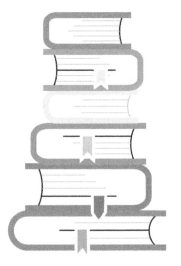

➢ **ASVAB Math Review** – Learn everything you need to know about the ASVAB Math test.

➢ **ASVAB Math Test-Taking Strategies** – Learn how to effectively put these recommended test-taking techniques into use for improving your ASVAB Math score.

➢ **Test Day Tips** – Review these tips to make sure you will do your best when the big day comes.

Effortless Math's ASVAB Online Center

Effortless Math Online ASVAB Center offers a complete study program, including the following:

✓ Step-by-step instructions on how to prepare for the ASVAB Math test

✓ Numerous ASVAB Math worksheets to help you measure your math skills

✓ Complete list of ASVAB Math formulas

✓ Video lessons for all ASVAB Math topics

✓ Full-length ASVAB Math practice tests

✓ And much more…

No Registration Required.

Visit **EffortlessMath.com/ASVAB** to find your online ASVAB Math resources.

How to Use This Book Effectively

L   ook no further when you need a study guide to improve your math skills to succeed on the math portion of the ASVAB test. Each chapter of this comprehensive guide to the ASVAB Math will provide you with the knowledge, tools, and understanding needed for every topic covered on the test.

It's imperative that you understand each topic before moving onto another one, as that's the way to guarantee your success. Each chapter provides you with examples and a step-by-step guide of every concept to better understand the content that will be on the test. To get the best possible results from this book:

➢ **Begin studying long before your test date**. This provides you ample time to learn the different math concepts. The earlier you begin studying for the test, the sharper your skills will be. Do not procrastinate! Provide yourself with plenty of time to learn the concepts and feel comfortable that you understand them when your test date arrives.

➢ **Practice consistently**. Study ASVAB Math concepts at least 20 to 30 minutes a day. Remember, slow and steady wins the race, which can be applied to preparing for the ASVAB Math test. Instead of cramming to tackle everything at once, be patient and learn the math topics in short bursts.

➢ Whenever you get a math problem wrong, **mark it off, and review it later** to make sure you understand the concept.

➢ Start each session by **looking over the previous material.**

➢ Once you've reviewed the book's lessons, **take a practice test** at the back of the book to gauge your level of readiness. Then, review your results. Read detailed answers and solutions for each question you missed.

➢ **Take another practice test** to get an idea of how ready you are to take the actual exam. Taking the practice tests will give you the confidence you need on test day. Simulate the ASVAB testing environment by sitting in a quiet room free from distraction. Make sure to clock yourself with a timer.

How to Study for the ASVAB Math Test

Studying for the ASVAB Math test can be a really daunting and boring task. What's the best way to go about it? Is there a certain study method that works better than others? Well, studying for the ASVAB Math can be done effectively. The following six-step program has been designed to make preparing for the ASVAB Math test more efficient and less overwhelming.

Step 1 - Create a study plan
Step 2 - Choose you study resources
Step 3 - Review, Learn, Practice
Step 4 - Learn and practice test-taking strategies
Step 5 - Learn the ASVAB Test format and take practice tests
Step 6 - Analyze your performance

STEP 1: Create a Study Plan

It's always easier to get things done when you have a plan. Creating a study plan for the ASVAB Math test can help you to stay on track with your studies. It's important to sit down and prepare a study plan with what works with your life, work, and any other obligations you may have. Devote enough time each day to studying. It's also a great idea to break down each section of the exam into blocks and study one concept at a time.

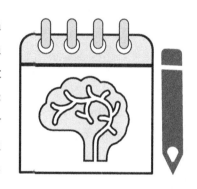

It's important to understand that there is no "right" way to create a study plan. Your study plan will be personalized based on your specific needs and learning style.

Follow these guidelines to create an effective study plan for your ASVAB Math test:

★ **Analyze your learning style and study habits** – Everyone has a different learning style. It is essential to embrace your individuality and the unique way you learn. Think about what works and what doesn't work for you. Do you prefer ASVAB Math prep books or a combination of textbooks and video lessons? Does it work better for you if you study every night for thirty minutes or is it more effective to study in the morning before going to work?

★ **Evaluate your schedule** – Review your current schedule and find out how much time you can consistently devote to ASVAB Math study.

★ **Develop a schedule** – Now it's time to add your study schedule to your calendar like any other obligation. Schedule time for study, practice, and review. Plan out which topic you will study on which day to ensure that you're devoting enough time to each concept. Develop a study plan that is mindful, realistic, and flexible.

★ **Stick to your schedule** – A study plan is only effective when it is followed consistently. You should try to develop a study plan that you can follow for the length of your study program.

★ **Evaluate your study plan and adjust as needed** – Sometimes you need to adjust your plan when you have new commitments. Check in with yourself regularly to make sure that you're not falling behind in your study plan. Remember, the most important thing is sticking to your plan. Your study plan is all about helping you be more productive. If you find that your study plan is not as effective as you want, don't get discouraged. It's okay to make changes as you figure out what works best for you.

STEP 2: Choose You Study Resources

There are numerous textbooks and online resources available for the ASVAB Math test, and it may not be clear where to begin. Don't worry! This study guide provides everything you need to fully prepare for your ASVAB Math test. In addition to the book content, you can also use Effortless Math's online resources. (video lessons, worksheets, formulas, etc.)

Simply visit <u>EffortlessMath.com/ASVAB</u> to find your online ASVAB Math resources.

STEP 3: Review, Learn, Practice

This ASVAB Math study guide breaks down each subject into specific skills or content areas. For instance, the percent concept is separated into different topics–percent calculation, percent increase and decrease, percent problems, etc. Use this book to help you go over all key math concepts and topics on the ASVAB Math test.

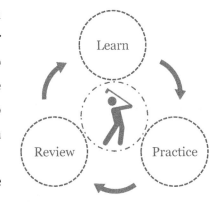

As you read each chapter, take notes or highlight the concepts you would like to go over again in the future. If you're unfamiliar with a topic or something is difficult for you, do additional research on it. For each math topic, plenty of instructions, step-by-step guides, and examples are provided to ensure you get a good grasp of the material. You can also find video lessons on the Effortless Math website for each ASVAB Math concept.

Quickly review the topics you do understand to get a brush-up of the material. Be sure to do the practice questions provided at the end of every chapter to measure your understanding of the concepts.

STEP 4: Learn and Practice Test-taking Strategies

In the following sections, you will find important test-taking strategies and tips that can help you earn extra points. You'll learn how to think strategically and when to guess if you don't know the answer to a question. Using ASVAB Math test-taking strategies and tips can help you raise your score and do well on the test. Apply test taking strategies on the practice tests to help you boost your confidence.

STEP 5: Learn the ASVAB Test Format and Take Practice Tests

The *ASVAB Test Review* section provides information about the structure of the ASVAB test. Read this section to learn more about the ASVAB test structure, different test sections, the number of questions in each section, and the section time limits. When you have a prior understanding of the test format and different types of ASVAB Math questions, you'll feel more confident when you take the actual exam.

Once you have read through the instructions and lessons and feel like you are ready to go – take advantage of both of the full-length ASVAB Math practice tests available in this study guide. Use the practice tests to sharpen your skills and build confidence.

The ASVAB Math practice tests offered at the end of the book are formatted similarly to the actual ASVAB Math test. When you take each practice test, try to simulate actual testing conditions. To take the practice tests, sit in a quiet space, time yourself, and work through as many of the questions as time allows. The practice tests are followed by detailed answer explanations to help you find your weak areas, learn from your mistakes, and raise your ASVAB Math score.

STEP 6: Analyze Your Performance

After taking the practice tests, look over the answer keys and explanations to learn which questions you answered correctly and which you did not. Never be discouraged if you make a few mistakes. See them as a learning opportunity. This will highlight your strengths and weaknesses.

You can use the results to determine if you need additional practice or if you are ready to take the actual ASVAB Math test.

Looking for more?

Visit EffortlessMath.com/ASVAB to find hundreds of ASVAB Math worksheets, video tutorials, practice tests, ASVAB Math formulas, and much more.

Or scan this QR code.

No Registration Required.

ASVAB TEST REVIEW

The Armed Services Vocational Aptitude Battery (ASVAB) was introduced in 1968. Over 40 million examinees have taken the ASVAB since then.

According to official ASVAB website, the ASVAB is a multiple-aptitude battery that measures developed abilities and helps predict future academic and occupational success in the military. It is administered annually to more than one million military applicants, high school, and post-secondary students.

ASVAB scores are reported as percentiles between 1-99. An ASVAB percentile score indicates the percentage of examinees in a reference group that scored at or below that particular score. For example, ASVAB score of 90 indicates that the examinee scored as well as or better than 90% of the nationally representative sample test takers. An ASVAB score of 60 indicates that the examinee scored as well as or better than 60% of the nationally representative sample.

There are three types of ASVAB:
- The CAT-ASVAB (computer adaptive test)
- The MET-site ASVAB (paper and pencil (P&P)
- The Student ASVAB (paper and pencil (P&P)

The CAT-ASVAB is a computer adaptive test. It means that if the correct answer is chosen, the next question will be harder. If the answer given is incorrect, the next question will be easier. This also means that once an answer is selected on the CAT it cannot be changed. The MET- site ASVAB and The Student ASVAB are paper and pencil (P&P) tests.

In this section, there are 2 complete Arithmetic Reasoning and Mathematics Knowledge ASVAB Tests. All practice tests are paper and pencil (P&P) ASVAB tests. Take these tests to see what score you'll be able to receive on a real ASVAB test.

ASVAB Math Test-Taking Strategies

Here are some test-taking strategies that you can use to maximize your performance and results on the ASVAB Math test.

#1: USE THIS APPROACH TO ANSWER EVERY ASVAB MATH QUESTION

- Review the question to identify keywords and important information.
- Translate the keywords into math operations so you can solve the problem.
- Review the answer choices. What are the differences between answer choices?
- Draw or label a diagram if needed.
- Try to find patterns.
- Find the right method to answer the question. Use straightforward math, plug in numbers, or test the answer choices (backsolving).
- Double-check your work.

#2: USE EDUCATED GUESSING

This approach is applicable to the problems you understand to some degree but cannot solve using straightforward math. In such cases, try to filter out as many answer choices as possible before picking an answer. In cases where you don't have a clue about what a certain problem entails, don't waste any time trying to eliminate answer choices. Just choose one randomly before moving onto the next question.

As you can ascertain, direct solutions are the most optimal approach. Carefully read through the question, determine what the solution is using the math you have learned before, then coordinate the answer with one of the choices available to you. Are you stumped? Make your best guess, then move on.

Don't leave any fields empty! Even if you're unable to work out a problem, strive to answer it. Take a guess if you have to. You will not lose points by getting an answer wrong, though you may gain a point by getting it correct!

#3: BALLPARK

A ballpark answer is a rough approximation. When we become overwhelmed by calculations and figures, we end up making silly mistakes. A decimal that is moved by one unit can change an answer from right to wrong, regardless of the number of steps that you went through to get it. That's where ballparking can play a big part.

If you think you know what the correct answer may be (even if it's just a ballpark answer), you'll usually have the ability to eliminate a couple of choices. While answer choices are usually based on the average student error and/or values that are closely tied, you will still be able to weed out choices that are way far afield. Try to find answers that aren't in the proverbial ballpark when you're looking for a wrong answer on a multiple-choice question. This is an optimal approach to eliminating answers to a problem.

#4: BACKSOLVING

All questions on the ASVAB Math test will be in multiple-choice format. Many test-takers prefer multiple-choice questions, as at least the answer is right there. You'll typically have four answers to pick from. You simply need to figure out which one is correct. Usually, the best way to go about doing so is "backsolving."

As mentioned earlier, direct solutions are the most optimal approach to answering a question. Carefully read through a problem, calculate a solution, then correspond the answer with one of the choices displayed in front of you. If you can't calculate a solution, your next best approach involves "backsolving."

When backsolving a problem, contrast one of your answer options against the problem you are asked, then see which of them is most relevant. More often than not, answer choices are listed in ascending or descending order. In such cases, try out the choices B or C. If it's not correct, you can go either down or up from there.

#5: PLUGGING IN NUMBERS

"Plugging in numbers" is a strategy that can be applied to a wide range of different math problems on the ASVAB Math test. This approach is typically used to simplify a challenging question so that it is more understandable. By using the strategy carefully, you can find the answer without too much trouble.

The concept is fairly straightforward–replace unknown variables in a problem with certain values. When selecting a number, consider the following:

- Choose a number that's basic (just not too basic). Generally, you should avoid choosing 1 (or even 0). A decent choice is 2.

- Try not to choose a number that is displayed in the problem.

- Make sure you keep your numbers different if you need to choose at least two of them.

- More often than not, choosing numbers merely lets you filter out some of your answer choices. As such, don't just go with the first choice that gives you the right answer.

- If several answers seem correct, then you'll need to choose another value and try again. This time, though, you'll just need to check choices that haven't been eliminated yet.

- If your question contains fractions, then a potential right answer may involve either an LCD (least common denominator) or an LCD multiple.

- 100 is the number you should choose when you are dealing with problems involving percentages.

ASVAB Mathematics Test – Daytime Tips

After practicing and reviewing all the math concepts you've been taught, and taking some ASVAB mathematics practice tests, you'll be prepared for test day. Consider the following tips to be extra-ready come test time.

Before Your Test

What to do the night before:

- **Relax!** One day before your test, study lightly or skip studying altogether. You shouldn't attempt to learn something new, either. There are plenty of reasons why studying the evening before a big test can work against you. Put it this way–a marathoner wouldn't go out for a sprint before the day of a big race. Mental marathoners–such as yourself– should not study for any more than one hour 24 hours before a ASVAB test. That's because your brain requires some rest to be at its best. The night before your exam, spend some time with family or friends, or read a book.

- **Avoid bright screens** - You'll have to get some good shuteye the night before your test. Bright screens (such as the ones coming from your laptop, TV, or mobile device) should be avoided altogether. Staring at such a screen will keep your brain up, making it hard to drift asleep at a reasonable hour.

- **Make sure your dinner is healthy** - The meal that you have for dinner should be nutritious. Be sure to drink plenty of water as well. Load up on your complex carbohydrates, much like a marathon runner would do. Pasta, rice, and potatoes are ideal options here, as are vegetables and protein sources.

- **Get your bag ready for test day** - The night prior to your test, pack your bag with your stationery, admissions pass, ID, and any other gear that you need. Keep the bag right by your front door.

- **Make plans to reach the testing site** - Before going to sleep, ensure that you understand precisely how you will arrive at the site of the test. If parking is something you'll have to find first, plan for it. If you're dependent on public transit, then review the schedule. You should also make sure that the train/bus/subway/streetcar you use will be running. Find out about road closures as well. If a parent or friend is accompanying you, ensure that they understand what steps they have to take as well.

The Day of the Test

- **Get up reasonably early, but not too early.**

- **Have breakfast** - Breakfast improves your concentration, memory, and mood. As such, make sure the breakfast that you eat in the morning is healthy. The last thing you want to be is distracted by a grumbling tummy. If it's not your own stomach making those noises, another test taker close to you might be instead. Prevent discomfort or embarrassment by consuming a healthy breakfast. Bring a snack with you if you think you'll need it.

- **Follow your daily routine** - Do you watch Good Morning America each morning while getting ready for the day? Don't break your usual habits on the day of the test. Likewise, if coffee isn't something you drink in the morning, then don't take up the habit hours before your test. Routine consistency lets you concentrate on the main objective–doing the best you can on your test.

- **Wear layers** - Dress yourself up in comfortable layers. You should be ready for any kind of internal temperature. If it gets too warm during the test, take a layer off.

- **Get there on time** - The last thing you want to do is get to the test site late. Rather, you should be there 45 minutes prior to the start of the test. Upon your arrival, try not to hang out with anybody who is nervous. Any anxious energy they exhibit shouldn't influence you.

- **Leave the books at home** - No books should be brought to the test site. If you start developing anxiety before the test, books could encourage you to do some last-minute studying, which will only hinder you. Keep the books far away–better yet, leave them at home.

- **Make your voice heard** - If something is off, speak to a proctor. If medical attention is needed or if you'll require anything, consult the proctor prior to the start of the test. Any doubts you have should be clarified. You should be entering the test site with a state of mind that is completely clear.

- **Have faith in yourself** - When you feel confident, you will be able to perform at your best. When you are waiting for the test to begin, envision yourself receiving an outstanding result. Try to see yourself as someone who knows all the answers, no matter what the questions are. A lot of athletes tend to use this technique–particularly before a big competition. Your expectations will be reflected by your performance.

During your test

- **Be calm and breathe deeply** - You need to relax before the test, and some deep breathing will go a long way to help you do that. Be confident and calm. You got this. Everybody feels a little stressed out just before an evaluation of any kind is set to begin. Learn some effective breathing exercises. Spend a minute meditating before the test starts. Filter out any negative thoughts you have. Exhibit confidence when having such thoughts.

- **Concentrate on the test** - Refrain from comparing yourself to anyone else. You shouldn't be distracted by the people near you or random noise. Concentrate exclusively on the test. If you find yourself irritated by surrounding noises, earplugs can be used to block sounds off close to you. Don't forget–the test is going to last several hours if you're taking more than one subject of the test. Some of that time will be dedicated to brief sections. Concentrate on the specific section you are working on during a particular moment. Do not let your mind wander off to upcoming or previous sections.

- **Skip challenging questions** - Optimize your time when taking the test. Lingering on a single question for too long will work against you. If you don't know what the answer is to a certain question, use your best guess, and move to the next question. There is no need to spend time attempting to solve something you aren't sure about. That time would be better served handling the questions you can actually answer well.

- **Try to answer each question individually** - Focus only on the question you are working on. Use one of the test-taking strategies to solve the problem. If you aren't able to come up with an answer, don't get frustrated. Simply skip that question, then move onto the next one.

- **Don't forget to breathe!** Whenever you notice your mind wandering, your stress levels boosting, or frustration brewing, take a thirty-second break. Shut your eyes, drop your pencil, breathe deeply, and let your shoulders relax. You will end up being more productive when you allow yourself to relax for a moment.

- **Optimize your breaks** - When break time comes, use the restroom, have a snack, and reactivate your energy for the subsequent section. Doing some stretches can help stimulate your blood flow.

After your test

- **Take it easy** - You will need to set some time aside to relax and decompress once the test has concluded. There is no need to stress yourself out about what you could've said, or what you may have done wrong. At this point, there's nothing you can do about it. Your energy and time would be better spent on something that will bring you happiness for the remainder of your day.

- **Redoing the test** - Did you pass the test? Congratulations! Your hard work paid off! Passing this test means that you are ready to apply to gain entrance into any of the military branches..

  If you have failed your test, though, don't worry! The test can be retaken. In such cases, you will need to follow the retake policy. You also need to re-register to take the exam again.

Contents

CHAPTER 1:

FRACTIONS AND MIXED NUMBERS

Math Topics that you'll learn in this chapter:

▶ Simplifying Fractions

▶ Adding and Subtracting Fractions

▶ Multiplying and Dividing Fractions

▶ Adding Mixed Numbers

▶ Subtracting Mixed Numbers

▶ Multiplying Mixed Numbers

▶ Dividing Mixed Numbers

Simplifying Fractions

☑ A fraction contains two numbers separated by a bar between them. The bottom number, called the denominator, is the total number of equally divided portions in one whole. The top number, called the numerator, is how many portions you have. And the bar represents the operation of division.

☑ Simplifying a fraction means reducing it to the lowest terms. To simplify a fraction, evenly divide both the top and bottom of the fraction by $2, 3, 5, 7$, etc.

☑ Continue until you can't go any further.

Examples:

Example 1. Simplify $\frac{12}{30}$

Solution: To simplify $\frac{12}{30}$, find a number that both 12 and 30 are divisible by. Both are divisible by 6. Then: $\frac{12}{30} = \frac{12 \div 6}{30 \div 6} = \frac{2}{5}$

Example 2. Simplify $\frac{64}{80}$

Solution: To simplify $\frac{64}{80}$, find a number that both 64 and 80 are divisible by. Both are divisible by 8 and 16. Then: $\frac{64}{80} = \frac{64 \div 8}{80 \div 8} = \frac{8}{10}$, 8 and 10 are divisible by 2, then: $\frac{8}{10} = \frac{4}{5}$ or $\frac{64}{80} = \frac{64 \div 16}{80 \div 16} = \frac{4}{5}$

Example 3. Simplify $\frac{20}{60}$

Solution: To simplify $\frac{20}{60}$, find a number that both 20 and 60 are divisible by. Both are divisible by 20, then: $\frac{20}{60} = \frac{20 \div 20}{60 \div 20} = \frac{1}{3}$

ADDING AND SUBTRACTING FRACTIONS

☑ For "like" fractions (fractions with the same denominator), add or subtract the numerators (top numbers) and write the answer over the common denominator (bottom numbers).

☑ Adding and Subtracting fractions with the same denominator:

$$\frac{a}{b} + \frac{c}{b} = \frac{a+c}{b} \qquad \frac{a}{b} - \frac{c}{b} = \frac{a-c}{b}$$

☑ Find equivalent fractions with the same denominator before you can add or subtract fractions with different denominators.

☑ Adding and Subtracting fractions with different denominators:

$$\frac{a}{b} + \frac{c}{d} = \frac{ad+bc}{bd} \qquad \frac{a}{b} - \frac{c}{d} = \frac{ad-bc}{bd}$$

Examples:

Example 1. Find the sum. $\frac{3}{4} + \frac{1}{3} =$

Solution: These two fractions are "unlike" fractions. (they have different denominators). Use this formula: $\frac{a}{b} + \frac{c}{d} = \frac{ad+cb}{bd}$

Then: $\frac{3}{4} + \frac{1}{3} = \frac{(3)(3)+(4)(1)}{4 \times 3} = \frac{9+4}{12} = \frac{13}{12}$

Example 2. Find the difference. $\frac{4}{5} - \frac{3}{7} =$

Solution: For "unlike" fractions, find equivalent fractions with the same denominator before you can add or subtract fractions with different denominators. Use this formula:

$\frac{a}{b} - \frac{c}{d} = \frac{ad-bc}{bd}$

$\frac{4}{5} - \frac{3}{7} = \frac{(4)(7)-(3)(5)}{5 \times 7} = \frac{28-15}{35} = \frac{13}{35}$

MULTIPLYING AND DIVIDING FRACTIONS

☑ Multiplying fractions: multiply the top numbers and multiply the bottom numbers. Simplify if necessary. $\frac{a}{b} \times \frac{c}{d} = \frac{a \times c}{b \times d}$

☑ Dividing fractions: Keep, Change, Flip

☑ Keep the first fraction, change the division sign to multiplication, and flip the numerator and denominator of the second fraction. Then, solve!

$$\frac{a}{b} \div \frac{c}{d} = \frac{a}{b} \times \frac{d}{c} = \frac{a \times d}{b \times c}$$

Examples:

Example 1. Multiply. $\frac{5}{8} \times \frac{2}{3} =$

Solution: Multiply the top numbers and multiply the bottom numbers.
$\frac{5}{8} \times \frac{2}{3} = \frac{5 \times 2}{8 \times 3} = \frac{10}{24}$, simplify: $\frac{10}{24} = \frac{10 \div 2}{24 \div 2} = \frac{5}{12}$

Example 2. Solve. $\frac{1}{3} \div \frac{4}{7} =$

Solution: Keep the first fraction, change the division sign to multiplication, and flip the numerator and denominator of the second fraction.
Then: $\frac{1}{3} \div \frac{4}{7} = \frac{1}{3} \times \frac{7}{4} = \frac{1 \times 7}{3 \times 4} = \frac{7}{12}$

Example 3. Calculate. $\frac{3}{5} \times \frac{2}{3} =$

Solution: Multiply the top numbers and multiply the bottom numbers.
$\frac{3}{5} \times \frac{2}{3} = \frac{3 \times 2}{5 \times 3} = \frac{6}{15}$, simplify: $\frac{6}{15} = \frac{6 \div 3}{15 \div 3} = \frac{2}{5}$

Example 4. Solve. $\frac{1}{4} \div \frac{5}{6} =$

Solution: Keep the first fraction, change the division sign to multiplication, and flip the numerator and denominator of the second fraction.
Then: $\frac{1}{4} \div \frac{5}{6} = \frac{1}{4} \times \frac{6}{5} = \frac{1 \times 6}{4 \times 5} = \frac{6}{20}$, simplify: $\frac{6}{20} = \frac{6 \div 2}{20 \div 2} = \frac{3}{10}$

ADDING MIXED NUMBERS

Use the following steps for adding mixed numbers:

☑ Add whole numbers of the mixed numbers.

☑ Add the fractions of the mixed numbers.

☑ Find the Least Common Denominator (LCD) if necessary.

☑ Add whole numbers and fractions.

☑ Write your answer in lowest terms.

Examples:

Example 1. Add mixed numbers. $3\frac{1}{3} + 1\frac{4}{5} =$

Solution: Let's rewriting our equation with parts separated, $3\frac{1}{3} + 1\frac{4}{5} = 3 + \frac{1}{3} + 1 + \frac{4}{5}$. Now, add whole number parts: $3 + 1 = 4$

Add the fraction parts $\frac{1}{3} + \frac{4}{5}$. Rewrite to solve with the equivalent fractions. $\frac{1}{3} + \frac{4}{5} = \frac{5}{15} + \frac{12}{15} = \frac{17}{15}$. The answer is an improper fraction (numerator is bigger than denominator). Convert the improper fraction into a mixed number: $\frac{17}{15} = 1\frac{2}{15}$. Now, combine the whole and fraction parts: $4 + 1\frac{2}{15} = 5\frac{2}{15}$

Example 2. Find the sum. $1\frac{2}{5} + 2\frac{1}{2} =$

Solution: Rewriting our equation with parts separated, $1 + \frac{2}{5} + 2 + \frac{1}{2}$. Add the whole number parts:

$1 + 2 = 3$. Add the fraction parts: $\frac{2}{5} + \frac{1}{2} = \frac{4}{10} + \frac{5}{10} = \frac{9}{10}$

Now, combine the whole and fraction parts: $3 + \frac{9}{10} = 3\frac{9}{10}$

SUBTRACT MIXED NUMBERS

Use these steps for subtracting mixed numbers.

☑ Convert mixed numbers into improper fractions. $a\frac{c}{b} = \frac{ab+c}{b}$

☑ Find equivalent fractions with the same denominator for unlike fractions. (fractions with different denominators)

☑ Subtract the second fraction from the first one. $\frac{a}{b} - \frac{c}{d} = \frac{ad-bc}{bd}$

☑ Write your answer in lowest terms.

☑ If the answer is an improper fraction, convert it into a mixed number.

Examples:

Example 1. Subtract. $3\frac{4}{5} - 1\frac{3}{4} =$

Solution: Convert mixed numbers into fractions: $3\frac{4}{5} = \frac{3\times5+4}{5} = \frac{19}{5}$ and $1\frac{3}{4} = \frac{1\times4+3}{4} = \frac{7}{4}$

These two fractions are "unlike" fractions. (they have different denominators). Find equivalent fractions with the same denominator. Use this formula: $\frac{a}{b} - \frac{c}{d} = \frac{ad-bc}{bd}$

$\frac{19}{5} - \frac{7}{4} = \frac{(19)(4)-(5)(7)}{5\times4} = \frac{76-35}{20} = \frac{41}{20}$, the answer is an improper fraction, convert it into a mixed number. $\frac{41}{20} = 2\frac{1}{20}$

Example 2. Subtract. $4\frac{3}{8} - 1\frac{1}{2} =$

Solution: Convert mixed numbers into fractions: $4\frac{3}{8} = \frac{4\times8+3}{8} = \frac{35}{8}$ and $1\frac{1}{2} = \frac{1\times2+1}{4} = \frac{3}{2}$

Find equivalent fractions: $\frac{3}{2} = \frac{12}{8}$. Then: $4\frac{3}{8} - 1\frac{1}{2} = \frac{35}{8} - \frac{12}{8} = \frac{23}{8}$

The answer is an improper fraction, convert it into a mixed number. $\frac{23}{8} = 2\frac{7}{8}$

MULTIPLYING MIXED NUMBERS

Use the following steps for multiplying mixed numbers:

☑ Convert the mixed numbers into fractions. $a\frac{c}{b} = a + \frac{c}{b} = \frac{ab+c}{b}$

☑ Multiply fractions. $\frac{a}{b} \times \frac{c}{d} = \frac{a \times c}{b \times d}$

☑ Write your answer in lowest terms.

☑ If the answer is an improper fraction (numerator is bigger than denominator), convert it into a mixed number.

Examples:

Example 1. Multiply. $3\frac{1}{3} \times 4\frac{1}{6} =$

Solution: Convert mixed numbers into fractions, $3\frac{1}{3} = \frac{3 \times 3 + 1}{3} = \frac{10}{3}$ and $4\frac{1}{6} = \frac{4 \times 6 + 1}{6} = \frac{25}{6}$

Apply the fractions rule for multiplication, $\frac{10}{3} \times \frac{25}{6} = \frac{10 \times 25}{3 \times 6} = \frac{250}{18}$

The answer is an improper fraction. Convert it into a mixed number. $\frac{250}{18} = 13\frac{8}{9}$

Example 2. Multiply. $2\frac{1}{2} \times 3\frac{2}{3} =$

Solution: Converting mixed numbers into fractions, $2\frac{1}{2} \times 3\frac{2}{3} = \frac{5}{2} \times \frac{11}{3}$

Apply the fractions rule for multiplication, $\frac{5}{2} \times \frac{11}{3} = \frac{5 \times 11}{2 \times 3} = \frac{55}{6} = 9\frac{1}{6}$

Example 3. Multiply mixed numbers. $2\frac{1}{3} \times 2\frac{1}{2} =$

Solution: Converting mixed numbers to fractions, $2\frac{1}{3} = \frac{7}{3}$ and $2\frac{1}{2} = \frac{5}{2}$. Multiply two fractions:

$$\frac{7}{3} \times \frac{5}{2} = \frac{7 \times 5}{3 \times 2} = \frac{35}{6} = 5\frac{5}{6}$$

DIVIDING MIXED NUMBERS

Use the following steps for dividing mixed numbers:

☑ Convert the mixed numbers into fractions. $a\frac{c}{b} = a + \frac{c}{b} = \frac{ab+c}{b}$

☑ Divide fractions: Keep, Change, Flip: Keep the first fraction, change the division sign to multiplication, and flip the numerator and denominator of the second fraction. Then, solve! $\frac{a}{b} \div \frac{c}{d} = \frac{a}{b} \times \frac{d}{c} = \frac{a \times d}{b \times c}$

☑ Write your answer in lowest terms.

☑ If the answer is an improper fraction (numerator is bigger than denominator), convert it into a mixed number.

Examples:

Example 1. Solve. $3\frac{2}{3} \div 2\frac{1}{2}$

Solution: Convert mixed numbers into fractions: $3\frac{2}{3} = \frac{3 \times 3 + 2}{3} = \frac{11}{3}$ and $2\frac{1}{2} = \frac{2 \times 2 + 1}{2} = \frac{5}{2}$

Keep, Change, Flip: $\frac{11}{3} \div \frac{5}{2} = \frac{11}{3} \times \frac{2}{5} = \frac{11 \times 2}{3 \times 5} = \frac{22}{15}$. The answer is an improper fraction. Convert it into a mixed number: $\frac{22}{15} = 1\frac{7}{15}$

Example 2. Solve. $3\frac{4}{5} \div 1\frac{5}{6}$

Solution: Convert mixed numbers to fractions, then solve:
$3\frac{4}{5} \div 1\frac{5}{6} = \frac{19}{5} \div \frac{11}{6} = \frac{19}{5} \times \frac{6}{11} = \frac{114}{55} = 2\frac{4}{55}$

Example 3. Solve. $2\frac{2}{7} \div 2\frac{3}{5}$

Solution: Converting mixed numbers to fractions: $3\frac{4}{5} \div 1\frac{5}{6} = \frac{16}{7} \div \frac{13}{5}$

Keep, Change, Flip: $\frac{16}{7} \div \frac{13}{5} = \frac{16}{7} \times \frac{5}{13} = \frac{16 \times 5}{7 \times 13} = \frac{80}{91}$

CHAPTER 1: PRACTICES

✍ Simplify each fraction.

1) $\frac{16}{24} =$

2) $\frac{28}{70} =$

3) $\frac{30}{105} =$

4) $\frac{40}{35} =$

5) $\frac{48}{56} =$

6) $\frac{6}{120} =$

7) $\frac{15}{100} =$

8) $\frac{45}{54} =$

✍ Find the sum or difference.

9) $\frac{4}{12} + \frac{3}{12} =$

10) $\frac{5}{4} + \frac{1}{12} =$

11) $\frac{3}{6} + \frac{2}{5} =$

12) $\frac{8}{25} - \frac{3}{25} =$

13) $\frac{5}{3} - \frac{2}{9} =$

14) $\frac{3}{2} - \frac{3}{4} =$

15) $\frac{4}{3} - \frac{6}{5} =$

16) $\frac{5}{12} + \frac{3}{5} =$

✍ Find the products or quotients.

17) $\frac{9}{5} \div \frac{3}{2} =$

18) $\frac{8}{7} \div \frac{4}{3} =$

19) $\frac{6}{4} \times \frac{8}{5} =$

20) $\frac{7}{2} \times \frac{4}{9} =$

✍ Find the sum.

21) $2\frac{1}{3} + 1\frac{4}{5} =$

22) $4\frac{3}{7} + 3\frac{3}{4} =$

23) $2\frac{3}{4} + 3\frac{1}{3} =$

24) $1\frac{1}{4} + 3\frac{1}{2} =$

25) $2\frac{5}{7} + 2\frac{1}{3} =$

26) $4\frac{2}{9} + 2\frac{1}{2} =$

✎ Find the difference.

27) $4\frac{2}{9} - 3\frac{1}{7} =$

28) $3\frac{3}{4} - 2\frac{1}{8} =$

29) $3\frac{2}{7} - 2\frac{4}{9} =$

30) $8\frac{3}{4} - 2\frac{1}{8} =$

31) $5\frac{5}{6} - 3\frac{1}{24} =$

32) $7\frac{3}{10} - 4\frac{4}{5} =$

33) $8\frac{1}{6} - 3\frac{2}{3} =$

34) $14\frac{9}{10} - 8\frac{4}{5} =$

✎ Find the products.

35) $2\frac{1}{9} \times 2\frac{5}{6} =$

36) $2\frac{3}{4} \times 4\frac{1}{9} =$

37) $1\frac{2}{7} \times 1\frac{5}{6} =$

38) $3\frac{2}{9} \times 1\frac{6}{5} =$

39) $3\frac{2}{3} \times 2\frac{3}{5} =$

40) $2\frac{5}{6} \times 3\frac{1}{9} =$

41) $3\frac{4}{5} \times 1\frac{1}{6} =$

42) $4\frac{1}{5} \times 1\frac{2}{7} =$

✎ Solve.

43) $8\frac{3}{4} \div 4\frac{1}{3} =$

44) $4\frac{2}{5} \div 1\frac{2}{9} =$

45) $6\frac{1}{2} \div 2\frac{1}{3} =$

46) $7\frac{1}{6} \div 3\frac{4}{9} =$

47) $2\frac{1}{4} \div 1\frac{1}{8} =$

48) $3\frac{2}{5} \div 1\frac{1}{10} =$

49) $4\frac{1}{2} \div 2\frac{2}{3} =$

50) $11\frac{1}{3} \div 2\frac{2}{9} =$

CHAPTER 1: ANSWERS

1) $\frac{2}{3}$

2) $\frac{2}{5}$

3) $\frac{2}{7}$

4) $\frac{8}{7}$

5) $\frac{6}{7}$

6) $\frac{1}{20}$

7) $\frac{3}{20}$

8) $\frac{5}{6}$

9) $\frac{7}{12}$

10) $\frac{4}{3}$

11) $\frac{9}{10}$

12) $\frac{1}{5}$

13) $\frac{13}{9} = 1\frac{4}{9}$

14) $\frac{3}{4}$

15) $\frac{2}{15}$

16) $\frac{61}{60} = 1\frac{1}{60}$

17) $\frac{6}{5}$

18) $\frac{6}{7}$

19) $\frac{12}{5} = 2\frac{2}{5}$

20) $\frac{14}{9} = 1\frac{5}{9}$

21) $4\frac{2}{15}$

22) $8\frac{5}{28}$

23) $6\frac{1}{12}$

24) $4\frac{3}{4}$

25) $5\frac{1}{21}$

26) $6\frac{13}{18}$

27) $1\frac{5}{63}$

28) $1\frac{5}{8}$

29) $\frac{53}{63}$

30) $6\frac{5}{8}$

31) $2\frac{19}{24}$

32) $2\frac{1}{2}$

33) $4\frac{1}{2}$

34) $6\frac{1}{10}$

35) $5\frac{53}{54}$

36) $11\frac{11}{36}$

37) $2\frac{5}{14}$

38) $7\frac{4}{45}$

39) $9\frac{8}{15}$

40) $8\frac{22}{27}$

41) $4\frac{13}{30}$

42) $5\frac{2}{5}$

43) $2\frac{1}{52}$

44) $3\frac{3}{5}$

45) $2\frac{11}{14}$

46) $2\frac{5}{62}$

47) 2

48) $3\frac{1}{11}$

49) $1\frac{11}{16}$

50) $5\frac{1}{10}$

CHAPTER 2:

DECIMALS

Math Topics that you'll learn in this chapter:

- ▶ Comparing Decimals
- ▶ Rounding Decimals
- ▶ Adding and Subtracting Decimals
- ▶ Multiplying and Dividing Decimals

COMPARING DECIMALS

✅ A decimal is a fraction written in a special form. For example, instead of writing $\frac{1}{2}$ you can write 0.5

✅ A Decimal Number contains a Decimal Point. It separates the whole number part from the fractional part of a decimal number.

✅ Let's review decimal place values: Example: 53.9861

5: tens	3: ones	9: tenths
8: hundredths	6: thousandths	1: tens thousandths

✅ To compare decimals, compare each digit of two decimals in the same place value. Start from left. Compare hundreds, tens, ones, tenth, hundredth, etc.

✅ To compare numbers, use these symbols:

Equal to =,	Less than <,	Greater than >
Greater than or equal ≥,	Less than or equal ≤	

Examples:

Example 1. Compare 0.60 and 0.06.

Solution: 0.60 is greater than 0.06, because the tenth place of 0.60 is 6, but the tenth place of 0.06 is zero. Then: 0.60 > 0.06

Example 2. Compare 0.0815 and 0.815.

Solution: 0.815 *is greater than* 0.0815, because the tenth place of 0.815 is 8, but the tenth place of 0.0815 is zero. Then: 0.0815 < 0.815

ROUNDING DECIMALS

☑ We can round decimals to a certain accuracy or number of decimal places. This is used to make calculations easier to do and results easier to understand when exact values are not too important.

☑ First, you'll need to remember your place values: For example: 12.4869

1: tens	2: ones	4: tenths
8: hundredths	6: thousandths	9: tens thousandths

☑ To round a decimal, first find the place value you'll round to.

☑ Find the digit to the right of the place value you're rounding to. If it is 5 or bigger, add 1 to the place value you're rounding to and remove all digits on its right side. If the digit to the right of the place value is less than 5, keep the place value and remove all digits on the right.

Examples:

Example 1. Round 1.9278 to the thousandth place value.

Solution: First, look at the next place value to the right, (tens thousandths). It's 8 and it is greater than 5. Thus add 1 to the digit in the thousandth place. The thousandth place is 7. $\rightarrow 7 + 1 = 8$, then,
The answer is 1.928

Example 2. Round 9.4126 to the nearest hundredth.

Solution: First, look at the digit to the right of hundredth (thousandths place value). It's 2 and it is less than 5, thus remove all the digits to the right of hundredth place. Then, the answer is 9.41

ADDING AND SUBTRACTING DECIMALS

☑ Line up the decimal numbers.

☑ Add zeros to have the same number of digits for both numbers if necessary.

☑ Remember your place values: For example: 73.5196

7: tens	3: ones	5: tenths
1: hundredths	9: thousandths	6: tens thousandths

☑ Add or subtract using column addition or subtraction.

Examples:

Example 1. Add. $1.8 + 3.12$

Solution: First, line up the numbers: $\begin{array}{r} 1.8 \\ + 3.12 \\ \hline \end{array}$ → Add a zero to have the same number of digits for both numbers. $\begin{array}{r} 1.80 \\ + 3.12 \\ \hline \end{array}$ → Start with the hundredths place: $0 + 2 = 2$, $\begin{array}{r} 1.80 \\ + 3.12 \\ \hline 2 \end{array}$ → Continue with tenths place: $8 + 1 = 9$, $\begin{array}{r} 1.80 \\ + 3.12 \\ \hline .92 \end{array}$ → Add the ones place: $3 + 1 = 4$, $\begin{array}{r} 1.80 \\ + 3.12 \\ \hline 4.92 \end{array}$

Example 2. Find the difference. $3.67 - 2.23$

Solution: First, line up the numbers: $\begin{array}{r} 3.67 \\ - 2.23 \\ \hline \end{array}$ → Start with the hundredths place: $7 - 3 = 4$, $\begin{array}{r} 3.67 \\ - 2.23 \\ \hline 4 \end{array}$ → Continue with tenths place. $6 - 2 = 4$, $\begin{array}{r} 3.67 \\ - 2.23 \\ \hline .44 \end{array}$ → Subtract the ones place. $3 - 2 = 1$, $\begin{array}{r} 3.67 \\ - 2.23 \\ \hline 1.44 \end{array}$

MULTIPLYING AND DIVIDING DECIMALS

For multiplying decimals:

☑ Ignore the decimal point and set up and multiply the numbers as you do with whole numbers.

☑ Count the total number of decimal places in both of the factors.

☑ Place the decimal point in the product.

For dividing decimals:

☑ If the divisor is not a whole number, move the decimal point to the right to make it a whole number. Do the same for the dividend.

☑ Divide similar to whole numbers.

Examples:

Example 1. Find the product. $0.81 \times 0.32 =$

Solution: Set up and multiply the numbers as you do with whole numbers. Line up the numbers: $\begin{array}{r} 81 \\ \times 32 \\ \hline \end{array}$ → Start with the ones place then continue with other digits → $\begin{array}{r} 81 \\ \times 32 \\ \hline 2,592 \end{array}$. Count the total number of decimal places in both of the factors. There are four decimals digits. (two for each factor 0.81 and 0.32) Then: $0.81 \times 0.32 = 0.2592$

Example 2. Find the quotient. $1.60 \div 0.4 =$

Solution: The divisor is not a whole number. Multiply it by 10 to get 4: → $0.4 \times 10 = 4$
Do the same for the dividend to get 16. → $1.60 \times 10 = 16$
Now, divide $16 \div 4 = 4$. The answer is 4.

CHAPTER 2: PRACTICES

✍ Compare. Use >, =, and <

1) 0.55 ☐ 0.055

2) 0.34 ☐ 0.33

3) 0.66 ☐ 0.59

4) 2.650 ☐ 2.65

5) 2.34 ☐ 2.67

6) 2.46 ☐ 2.05

7) 0.16 ☐ 0.025

8) 5.05 ☐ 50.5

9) 1.020 ☐ 1.02

10) 3.022 ☐ 3.3

11) 1.400 ☐ 1.60

12) 3.44 ☐ 4.3

13) 0.380 ☐ 3.03

14) 2.081 ☐ 2.63

✍ Round each decimal to the nearest whole number.

15) 10.57

16) 4.8

17) 29.7

18) 32.58

19) 7.5

20) 8.87

21) 56.23

22) 6.39

23) 18.63

24) 25.56

25) 28.49

26) 12.67

27) 49.9

28) 17.77

29) 3.44

30) 55.56

✍ Find the sum or difference.

31) $25.31 + 56.37 =$

32) $78.32 - 65.10 =$

33) $65.80 + 14.26 =$

34) $90.24 - 53.81 =$

35) $76.41 - 49.27 =$

36) $45.39 + 17.86 =$

37) $56.02 + 30.60 =$

38) $67.01 - 28.40 =$

39) $75.14 - 25.96 =$

40) $37.52 + 13.50 =$

41) $84.71 - 54.18 =$

42) $24.12 + 29.84 =$

43) $50.59 - 46.25 =$

44) $63.13 + 21.14 =$

45) $45.23 - 35.17 =$

46) $18.02 + 30.40 =$

✍ Find the product or quotient.

47) $1.4 \times 3.2 =$

48) $8.2 \div 0.2 =$

49) 4.12×3.5

50) $6.8 \div 1.7 =$

51) $5.8 \times 0.5 =$

52) $1.54 \div 0.5 =$

53) $1.4 \times 3.2 =$

54) $5.8 \div 0.2 =$

55) $6.4 \times 7.3 =$

56) $0.3 \times 3.2 =$

57) $7.5 \times 5.6 =$

58) $45.6 \div 0.8 =$

59) $1.9 \times 5.8 =$

60) $6.74 \times 2.5 =$

61) $56.08 \div 0.2 =$

62) $36.2 \times 3.6 =$

CHAPTER 2: ANSWERS

1) >	22) 6	43) 4.34
2) >	23) 19	44) 84.27
3) >	24) 26	45) 10.06
4) =	25) 28	46) 48.42
5) <	26) 13	47) 4.48
6) >	27) 50	48) 41
7) >	28) 18	49) 14.42
8) <	29) 3	50) 4
9) =	30) 56	51) 2.9
10) <	31) 81.68	52) 3.08
11) <	32) 13.22	53) 4.48
12) <	33) 80.06	54) 29
13) <	34) 36.43	55) 46.72
14) <	35) 27.14	56) 0.96
15) 11	36) 63.25	57) 42
16) 5	37) 86.62	58) 57
17) 30	38) 38.61	59) 11.02
18) 33	39) 49.18	60) 16.85
19) 8	40) 51.02	61) 280.4
20) 9	41) 30.53	62) 130.32
21) 56	42) 53.96	

CHAPTER 3:

INTEGERS AND ORDER OF OPERATIONS

Math Topics that you'll learn in this chapter:

▶ Adding and Subtracting Integers

▶ Multiplying and Dividing Integers

▶ Order of Operations

▶ Integers and Absolute Value

ADDING AND SUBTRACTING INTEGERS

☑ Integers include zero, counting numbers, and the negative of the counting numbers. $\{\dots, -3, -2, -1, 0, 1, 2, 3, \dots\}$

☑ Add a positive integer by moving to the right on the number line. (you will get a bigger number)

☑ Add a negative integer by moving to the left on the number line. (you will get a smaller number)

☑ Subtract an integer by adding its opposite.

Examples:

Example 1. Solve. $(-4) - (-5) =$

Solution: Keep the first number and convert the sign of the second number to its opposite. (change subtraction into addition. Then: $(-4) + 5 = 1$

Example 2. Solve. $11 + (8 - 19) =$

Solution: First, subtract the numbers in brackets, $8 - 19 = -11$.
Then: $11 + (-11) = \rightarrow$ change addition into subtraction: $11 - 11 = 0$

Example 3. Solve. $5 - (-14 - 3) =$

Solution: First, subtract the numbers in brackets, $-14 - 3 = -17$
Then: $5 - (-17) = \rightarrow$ change subtraction into addition: $5 + 17 = 22$

Example 4. Solve. $10 + (-6 - 15) =$

Solution: First, subtract the numbers in brackets, $-6 - 15 = -21$
Then: $10 + (-21) = \rightarrow$ change addition into subtraction: $10 - 21 = -11$

MULTIPLYING AND DIVIDING INTEGERS

Use the following rules for multiplying and dividing integers:

☑ (negative) × (negative) = positive

☑ (negative) ÷ (negative) = positive

☑ (negative) × (positive) = negative

☑ (negative) ÷ (positive) = negative

☑ (positive) × (positive) = positive

☑ (positive) ÷ (negative) = negative

Examples:

Example 1. Solve. $2 \times (-3) =$

Solution: Use this rule: (positive) × (negative) = negative.
Then: $(2) \times (-3) = -6$

Example 2. Solve. $(-5) + (-27 \div 9) =$

Solution: First, divide −27 by 9, the numbers in brackets, use this rule:
(negative) ÷ (positive) = negative. Then: $-27 \div 9 = -3$
$(-5) + (-27 \div 9) = (-5) + (-3) = -5 - 3 = -8$

Example 3. Solve. $(15 - 17) \times (-8) =$

Solution: First, subtract the numbers in brackets,
$15 - 17 = -2 \rightarrow (-2) \times (-8) =$
Now use this rule: (negative) × (negative) = positive $\rightarrow (-2) \times (-8) = 16$

Example 4. Solve. $(16 - 10) \div (-2) =$

Solution: First, subtract the numbers in brackets,
$16 - 10 = 6 \rightarrow (6) \div (-2) =$
Now use this rule: (positive) ÷ (negative) = negative $\rightarrow (6) \div (-2) = -3$

ORDER OF OPERATIONS

☑ In Mathematics, "operations" are addition, subtraction, multiplication, division, exponentiation (written as b^n), and grouping;

☑ When there is more than one math operation in an expression, use PEMDAS: (to memorize this rule, remember the phrase "Please Excuse My Dear Aunt Sally".)

- ❖ Parentheses
- ❖ Exponents
- ❖ Multiplication and Division (from left to right)
- ❖ Addition and Subtraction (from left to right)

Examples:

Example 1. Calculate. $(3 + 5) \div (3^2 \div 9) =$

Solution: First, simplify inside parentheses:
$(8) \div (9 \div 9) = (8) \div (1)$, Then: $(8) \div (1) = 8$

Example 2. Solve. $(7 \times 8) - (12 - 4) =$

Solution: First, calculate within parentheses: $(7 \times 8) - (12 - 4) =$
$(56) - (8)$, Then: $(56) - (8) = 48$

Example 3. Calculate. $-2[(8 \times 9) \div (2^2 \times 2)] =$

Solution: First, calculate within parentheses:
$-2[(72) \div (4 \times 2)] = -2[(72) \div (8)] = -2[9]$
multiply -2 and 9. Then: $-2[9] = -18$

Example 4. Solve. $(14 \div 7) + (-13 + 8) =$

Solution: First, calculate within parentheses:
$(14 \div 7) + (-13 + 8) = (2) + (-5)$ Then: $(2) - (5) = -3$

INTEGERS AND ABSOLUTE VALUE

☑ The absolute value of a number is its distance from zero, in either direction, on the number line. For example, the distance of 9 and −9 from zero on number line is 9.

☑ The absolute value of an integer is the numerical value without its sign. (negative or positive)

☑ The vertical bar is used for absolute value as in $|x|$.

☑ The absolute value of a number is never negative; because it only shows, "how far the number is from zero".

Examples:

Example 1. Calculate. $|12 − 4| × 4 =$

Solution: First, solve $|12 − 4|$, $→|12 − 4| = |8|$, the absolute value of 8 is 8, $|8| = 8$ Then: $8 × 4 = 32$

Example 2. Solve. $\frac{|-16|}{4} × |3 − 8| =$

Solution: First, find $|-16|$, $→$ the absolute value of −16 is 16,
Then: $|-16| = 16$, $\frac{16}{4} × |3 − 8| =$

Now, calculate $|3 − 8|$, $→ |3 − 8| = |-5|$, the absolute value of −5 is 5. $|-5| = 5$ then: $\frac{16}{4} × 5 = 4 × 5 = 20$

Example 3. Solve. $|9 − 3| × \frac{|-3×8|}{6} =$

Solution: First, calculate $|9 − 3|$, $→|9 − 3| = |6|$, the absolute value of 6 is 6, $|6| = 6$. Then: $6 × \frac{|-3×8|}{6}$

Now calculate $|-3 × 8|$, $→ |-3 × 8| = |-24|$, the absolute value of −24 is 24, $|-24| = 24$ Then: $6 × \frac{24}{6} = 6 × 4 = 24$

CHAPTER 3: PRACTICES

✎ Find each sum or difference.

1) $13 - (-6) =$

2) $(-36) + 18 =$

3) $(-6) + (-22) =$

4) $54 + (-12) + 9 =$

5) $35 + (-24 + 4) =$

6) $(-17) + (-34 + 12) =$

7) $(-1) + (28 - 15) =$

8) $5 + (-9 + 12) =$

9) $(-10) + (-20) =$

10) $32 - (-5) =$

11) $(-9) + (24 - 3) =$

12) $8 - (-2 + 12) =$

13) $(-3) + (45 + 3) =$

14) $5 + (-30 + 6) =$

15) $(-6 + 1) + (-20) =$

16) $(-7) - (-20 + 2) =$

17) $(-6) - (2) =$

18) $(9 - 6) - (-3) =$

✎ Solve.

19) $4 \times (-8) =$

20) $(-27) \div (-9) =$

21) $(-2) \times (-9) \times 3 =$

22) $5 \times (-3) \times (-7) =$

23) $(-10 - 8) \div (-9) =$

24) $(-9 + 7) \times (-20) =$

25) $(-7) \times (-5) =$

26) $(-6) \times (-2 + 6) =$

27) $(-3) \times (-4) \times 3 =$

28) $(-8 - 2) \times (-1 + 4) =$

29) $(-9) \times (-20) =$

30) $6 \times (-2 + 9) =$

31) $(-5 - 6) \times (-2) =$

32) $(-4 - 2) \times (-3 - 7) =$

33) $(-9) \div (13 - 16) =$

34) $56 \times (-8) =$

35) $(-9 - 3) \div (-4) =$

36) $72 \div (-18 + 10) =$

✍ Evaluate each expression.

37) $2 + (6 \times 4) =$

38) $(7 \times 9) - 8 =$

39) $(-6) + (2 \times 9) =$

40) $(-2 - 4) + (3 \times 7) =$

41) $(28 \div 7) - (5 \times 3) =$

42) $(9 \times 3) + (6 \times 4) =$

43) $(36 \div 4) - (36 \div 6) =$

44) $(7 + 3) + (16 \div 2) =$

45) $(15 \times 3) - 16 =$

46) $8 - (7 \times 3) =$

47) $(9 + 15) \div (8 \div 4) =$

48) $2[(3 \times 6) + (16 \times 2)] =$

49) $(18 - 6) + (4 \times 2) =$

50) $2[(2 \times 3) - (8 \times 5)] =$

51) $(9 + 7) \div (16 \div 8) =$

52) $(3 + 9) \times (25 \times 2) =$

53) $3[(10 \times 9) \div (9 \times 5)] =$

54) $-6[(10 \times 9) \div (5 \times 6)] =$

✍ Find the answers.

55) $|-8| + |6 - 15| =$

56) $|-5 + 9| + |-3| =$

57) $|-6| + |2 - 10| =$

58) $|-8 + 3| - |4 - 8| =$

59) $|6 - 10| + |5 - 7| =$

60) $|-6| - |-9 - 19| + 5 =$

61) $|-9 + 2| - |3 - 5| + 6 =$

62) $4 + |3 - 7| + |2 - 6| =$

63) $\dfrac{|-64|}{8} \times \dfrac{|-48|}{6} =$

64) $\dfrac{|-36|}{6} \times \dfrac{|-56|}{8} =$

65) $\dfrac{|-72|}{9} \times \dfrac{|-45|}{5} =$

66) $|8 \times (-1)| \times \dfrac{|-24|}{3} =$

67) $|-2 \times 5| \times \dfrac{|-27|}{9} =$

68) $\dfrac{|-144|}{12} - |-6 \times 4| =$

69) $\dfrac{|-63|}{7} + |-9 \times 2| =$

70) $\dfrac{|-70|}{7} + |-8 \times 3| =$

71) $\dfrac{|-7 \times -3|}{7} \times \dfrac{|8 \times (-5)|}{8} =$

72) $\dfrac{|(-2) \times (-6)|}{4} \times \dfrac{|8 \times (-4)|}{2} =$

CHAPTER 3: ANSWERS

1) 19
2) −18
3) −28
4) 51
5) 15
6) −39
7) 12
8) 8
9) −30
10) 37
11) 12
12) −2
13) 45
14) −19
15) −25
16) 11
17) −8
18) 6
19) −32
20) 3
21) 54
22) 105
23) 2
24) 40

25) 35
26) −24
27) 36
28) −30
29) 180
30) 42
31) 22
32) 60
33) 3
34) −448
35) 3
36) −9
37) 26
38) 55
39) 12
40) 15
41) −11
42) 51
43) 3
44) 18
45) 29
46) −13
47) 12
48) 100

49) 20
50) −68
51) 8
52) 600
53) 6
54) −18
55) 17
56) 7
57) 14
58) 1
59) 6
60) −17
61) 11
62) 12
63) 64
64) 42
65) 72
66) 64
67) 30
68) −12
69) 27
70) 34
71) 15
72) 48

CHAPTER 4:
RATIOS AND PROPORTIONS

Math Topics that you'll learn in this chapter:

▶ Simplifying Ratios

▶ Proportional Ratios

▶ Similarity and Ratios

SIMPLIFYING RATIOS

- ☑ Ratios are used to make comparisons between two numbers.

- ☑ Ratios can be written as a fraction, using the word "to", or with a colon. Example: $\frac{3}{4}$ or "3 to 4" or $3:4$

- ☑ You can calculate equivalent ratios by multiplying or dividing both sides of the ratio by the same number.

Examples:

Example 1. Simplify. $9:3 =$

Solution: Both numbers 9 and 3 are divisible by 3 , $\Rightarrow 9 \div 3 = 3$, $3 \div 3 = 1$, Then: $9:3 = 3:1$

Example 2. Simplify. $\frac{24}{44} =$

Solution: Both numbers 24 and 44 are divisible by 4, $\Rightarrow 24 \div 4 = 6$, $44 \div 4 = 11$, Then: $\frac{24}{44} = \frac{6}{11}$

Example 3. There are 36 students in a class and 16 are girls. Write the ratio of girls to boys.

Solution: Subtract 16 from 36 to find the number of boys in the class. $36 - 16 = 20$. There are 20 boys in the class. So, the ratio of girls to boys is $16:20$. Now, simplify this ratio. Both 20 and 16 are divisible by 4. Then: $20 \div 4 = 5$, and $16 \div 4 = 4$. In the simplest form, this ratio is $4:5$

Example 4. A recipe calls for butter and sugar in the ratio $3:4$. If you're using 9 cups of butter, how many cups of sugar should you use?

Solution: Since you use 9 cups of butter, or 3 times as much, you need to multiply the amount of sugar by 3. Then: $4 \times 3 = 12$. So, you need to use 12 cups of sugar. You can solve this using equivalent fractions: $\frac{3}{4} = \frac{9}{12}$

Proportional Ratios

☑ Two ratios are proportional if they represent the same relationship.

☑ A proportion means that two ratios are equal. It can be written in two ways:

$$\frac{a}{b} = \frac{c}{d} \qquad a : b = c : d$$

☑ The proportion $\frac{a}{b} = \frac{c}{d}$ can be written as: $a \times d = c \times b$

Examples:

Example 1. Solve this proportion for x. $\quad \frac{3}{7} = \frac{12}{x}$

Solution: Use cross multiplication: $\frac{3}{7} = \frac{12}{x} \Rightarrow 3 \times x = 7 \times 12 \Rightarrow 3x = 84$

Divide both sides by 3 to find x: $\qquad x = \frac{84}{3} \Rightarrow x = 28$

Example 2. If a box contains red and blue balls in ratio of $3 : 7$ red to blue, how many red balls are there if 49 blue balls are in the box?

Solution: Write a proportion and solve. $\frac{3}{7} = \frac{x}{49}$

Use cross multiplication: $\qquad 3 \times 49 = 7 \times x \Rightarrow 147 = 7x$

Divide to find x: $x = \frac{147}{7} \Rightarrow x = 21$. There are 21 red balls in the box.

Example 3. Solve this proportion for x. $\quad \frac{2}{9} = \frac{12}{x}$

Solution: Use cross multiplication: $\frac{2}{9} = \frac{12}{x} \Rightarrow 2 \times x = 9 \times 12 \Rightarrow 2x = 108$

Divide to find x: $x = \frac{108}{2} \Rightarrow x = 54$

Example 4. Solve this proportion for x. $\frac{6}{7} = \frac{18}{x}$

Solution: Use cross multiplication: $\frac{6}{7} = \frac{18}{x} \Rightarrow 6 \times x = 7 \times 18 \Rightarrow 6x = 126$

Divide to find x: $x = \frac{126}{6} \Rightarrow x = 21$

SIMILARITY AND RATIOS

☑ Two figures are similar if they have the same shape.

☑ Two or more figures are similar if the corresponding angles are equal, and the corresponding sides are in proportion.

Examples:

Example 1. The following triangles are similar. What is the value of the unknown side?

Solution: Find the corresponding sides and write a proportion.
$\frac{5}{10} = \frac{4}{x}$. Now, use the cross product to solve for x:
$\frac{5}{10} = \frac{4}{x} \to 5 \times x = 10 \times 4 \to 5x = 40$. Divide both sides by 5. Then: $5x = 40 \to \frac{5x}{5} = \frac{40}{5} \to x = 8$
The missing side is 8.

Example 2. Two rectangles are similar. The first is 6 feet wide and 20 feet long. The second is 15 feet wide. What is the length of the second rectangle?

Solution: Let's put x for the length of the second rectangle. Since two rectangles are similar, their corresponding sides are in proportion. Write a proportion and solve for the missing number.
$\frac{6}{15} = \frac{20}{x} \to 6x = 15 \times 20 \to 6x = 300 \to x = \frac{300}{6} = 50$
The length of the second rectangle is 50 feet.

CHAPTER 4: PRACTICES

✍ Reduce each ratio.

1) $3 : 21 = $ ___ : ___

2) $8 : 72 = $ ___ : ___

3) $21 : 49 = $ ___ : ___

4) $32 : 28 = $ ___ : ___

5) $35 : 45 = $ ___ : ___

6) $72 : 81 = $ ___ : ___

7) $36 : 54 = $ ___ : ___

8) $56 : 64 = $ ___ : ___

9) $12 : 36 = $ ___ : ___

10) $4 : 32 = $ ___ : ___

11) $16 : 48 = $ ___ : ___

12) $15 : 105 = $ ___ : ___

✍ Solve.

13) Bob has 18 red cards and 27 green cards. What is the ratio of Bob's red cards to his green cards? _____

14) In a party, 30 soft drinks are required for every 18 guests. If there are 240 guests, how many soft drinks are required? _____

15) Sara has 72 blue pens and 36 black pens. What is the ratio of Sara's black pens to her blue pens? _____

16) In Jack's class, 45 of the students are tall and 18 are short. In Michael's class 27 students are tall and 12 students are short. Which class has a higher ratio of tall to short students? _____

17) The price of 3 apples at the Quick Market is $1.44. The price of 5 of the same apples at Walmart is $2.45. Which place is the better buy? _____

18) The bakers at a Bakery can make 160 bagels in 4 hours. How many bagels can they bake in 14 hours? What is that rate per hour? _____

19) You can buy 5 cans of green beans at a supermarket for $3.40. How much does it cost to buy 35 cans of green beans? _____

✍ Solve each proportion.

20) $\frac{3}{4} = \frac{15}{x}$, $x =$

21) $\frac{9}{6} = \frac{x}{4}$, $x =$ _____

22) $\frac{3}{15} = \frac{2}{x}$, $x =$ _____

23) $\frac{5}{15} = \frac{3}{x}$, $x =$ _____

24) $\frac{24}{3} = \frac{x}{2}$, $x =$ _____

25) $\frac{8}{12} = \frac{10}{x}$, $x =$ _____

26) $\frac{3}{x} = \frac{2}{14}$, $x =$ _____

27) $\frac{10}{x} = \frac{3}{6}$, $x =$ _____

28) $\frac{15}{6} = \frac{x}{4}$, $x =$ _____

29) $\frac{x}{12} = \frac{5}{10}$, $x =$ _____

30) $\frac{18}{6} = \frac{3}{x}$, $x =$ _____

31) $\frac{3}{4} = \frac{24}{x}$, $x =$ _____

32) $\frac{8}{4} = \frac{x}{2}$, $x =$ _____

33) $\frac{12}{3} = \frac{x}{4}$, $x =$ _____

34) $\frac{24}{8} = \frac{x}{2}$, $x =$ _____

35) $\frac{5}{3} = \frac{x}{6}$, $x =$ _____

36) $\frac{10}{8} = \frac{x}{4}$, $x =$ _____

37) $\frac{x}{6} = \frac{6}{4}$, $x =$ _____

38) $\frac{x}{4} = \frac{7}{2}$, $x =$ _____

39) $\frac{9}{x} = \frac{3}{4}$, $x =$ _____

40) $\frac{10}{x} = \frac{1}{5}$, $x =$ _____

41) $\frac{9}{2} = \frac{x}{8}$, $x =$ _____

✍ Solve each problem.

42) Two rectangles are similar. The first is 6 feet wide and 24 feet long. The second is 10 *feet* wide. What is the length of the second rectangle?

_____

43) Two rectangles are similar. One is 4.8 meters by 6 meters. The longer side of the second rectangle is 27 *meters*. What is the other side of the second rectangle? _____

CHAPTER 4: ANSWERS

1) $1:7$
2) $1:9$
3) $3:7$
4) $8:7$
5) $7:9$
6) $8:9$
7) $2:3$
8) $7:8$
9) $1:3$
10) $1:8$
11) $1:3$
12) $1:7$
13) $2:3$
14) 400
15) $1:2$
16) $Jack's\ class = \frac{45}{18} = \frac{5}{2}$

$Michael's\ class = \frac{27}{12} = \frac{9}{4}$

Jack's class has a higher ratio of tall to short student
17) Quick Market
18) 560
19) $\$23.80$
20) 20

21) 6
22) 10
23) 9
24) 16
25) 15
26) 21
27) 20
28) 10
29) 6
30) 1
31) 32
32) 4
33) 16
34) 6
35) 10
36) 5
37) 9
38) 14
39) 12
40) 50
41) 36
42) 40
43) $21.6\ meters$

CHAPTER 5:

PERCENTAGE

Math Topics that you'll learn in this chapter:

▶ Percentage Calculations

▶ Percent Problems

▶ Percent of Increase and Decrease

▶ Discount, Tax and Tip

▶ Simple Interest

PERCENT PROBLEMS

✔ Percent is a ratio of a number and 100. It always has the same denominator, 100. The percent symbol is "%".

✔ Percent means "per 100". So, 20% is $\frac{20}{100}$.

✔ In each percent problem, we are looking for the base, or part or the percent.

✔ Use these equations to find each missing section in a percent problem:

   ❖ Base = Part ÷ Percent

   ❖ Part = Percent × Base

   ❖ Percent = Part ÷ Base

Examples:

Example 1. What is 25% of 60?

Solution: In this problem, we have percent (25%) and base (60) and we are looking for the "part". Use this formula: *part = percent × base*.
Then: $part = 25\% \times 60 = \frac{25}{100} \times 60 = 0.25 \times 60 = 15$. The answer: 25% of 60 is 15.

Example 2. 20 is what percent of 400?

Solution: In this problem, we are looking for the percent. Use this equation: *Percent = Part ÷ Base → Percent = 20 ÷ 400 = 0.05 = 5%*.
Then: 20 is 5 percent of 400.

PERCENT OF INCREASE AND DECREASE

☑ Percent of change (increase or decrease) is a mathematical concept that represents the degree of change over time.

☑ To find the percentage of increase or decrease:

1. New Number – Original Number

2. The result ÷ Original Number × 100

☑ Or use this formula: Percent of change $= \frac{new\ number - original\ number}{original\ number} \times 100$

☑ Note: If your answer is a negative number, then this is a percentage decrease. If it is positive, then this is a percentage increase.

Examples:

Example 1. The price of a shirt increases from $20 to $30. What is the percentage increase?

Solution: First, find the difference: $30 - 20 = 10$

Then: $10 \div 20 \times 100 = \frac{10}{20} \times 100 = 50$. The percentage increase is 50. It means that the price of the shirt increased by 50%.

Example 2. The price of a table increased from $25 to $40. What is the percent of increase?

Solution: Use percentage formula:

$Percent\ of\ change = \frac{new\ number - original\ number}{original\ number} \times 100 =$

$\frac{40-25}{25} \times 100 = \frac{15}{25} \times 100 = 0.6 \times 100 = 60$. The percentage increase is 60. It means that the price of the table increased by 60%.

DISCOUNT, TAX AND TIP

☑ To find the discount: Multiply the regular price by the rate of discount

☑ To find the selling price: Original price – discount

☑ To find tax: Multiply the tax rate to the taxable amount (income, property value, etc.)

☑ To find the tip, multiply the rate to the selling price.

Examples:

Example 1. With an 10% discount, Ella saved $45 on a dress. What was the original price of the dress?

Solution: let x be the original price of the dress. Then: $10\% \ of \ x = 45$. Write an equation and solve for x: $0.10 \times x = 45 \rightarrow x = \frac{45}{0.10} = 450$. The original price of the dress was $450.

Example 2. Sophia purchased a new computer for a price of $950 at the Apple Store. What is the total amount her credit card is charged if the sales tax is 7%?

Solution: The taxable amount is $950, and the tax rate is 7%. Then: $Tax = 0.07 \times 950 = 66.50$
$Final \ price = Selling \ price + Tax \rightarrow final \ price = \$950 + \$66.50 = \$1,016.50$

Example 3. Nicole and her friends went out to eat at a restaurant. If their bill was $80.00 and they gave their server a 15% tip, how much did they pay altogether?

Solution: First, find the tip. To find the tip, multiply the rate to the bill amount. $Tip = 80 \times 0.15 = 12$. The final price is: $\$80 + \$12 = \$92$

SIMPLE INTEREST

☑ Simple Interest: The charge for borrowing money or the return for lending it.

☑ Simple interest is calculated on the initial amount (principal).

☑ To solve a simple interest problem, use this formula:

Interest = principal × rate × time $(I = p \times r \times t = prt)$

Examples:

Example 1. Find simple interest for $300 investment at 6% for 5 years.

Solution: Use Interest formula:
$I = prt$ ($P = \$300$, r = 6% = $\frac{6}{100}$ = 0.06 and $t = 5$)
Then: $I = 300 \times 0.06 \times 5 = \$90$

Example 2. Find simple interest for $1,600 at 5% for 2 years.

Solution: Use Interest formula:
$I = prt$ ($P = \$1,600$, r = 5% = $\frac{5}{100}$ = 0.05 and $t = 2$)
Then: $I = 1,600 \times 0.05 \times 2 = \$160$

Example 3. Andy received a student loan to pay for his educational expenses this year. What is the interest on the loan if he borrowed $6,500 at 8% for 6 years?

Solution: Use Interest formula:$I = prt$. $P = \$6,500$, r = 8% = 0.08 and $t = 6$. Then: $I = 6,500 \times 0.08 \times 6 = \$3,120$

Example 4. Bob is starting his own small business. He borrowed $10,000 from the bank at a 6% rate for 6 months. Find the interest Bob will pay on this loan.

Solution: Use Interest formula:
$I = prt$. $P = \$10,000$, $r = 6\% = 0.06$ and $t = 0.5$ (6 months is half year).
Then: $I = 10,000 \times 0.06 \times 0.5 = \$300$

CHAPTER 5: PRACTICES

✎ Solve each problem.

1) 10 is what percent of 80? ____%

2) 12 is what percent of 60? ____%

3) 20 is what percent of 80? ____%

4) 18 is what percent of 72? ____%

5) 16 is what percent of 50? ____%

6) 35 is what percent of 140? ____%

7) 12 is what percent of 240? ____%

8) 80 is what percent of 400? ____%

9) 60 is what percent of 300? ____%

10) 100 is what percent of 250? ____%

11) 25 is what percent of 400? ____%

12) 60 is what percent of 480? ____%

✎ Solve each problem.

13) Bob got a raise, and his hourly wage increased from $16 to $20. What is the percent increase? _____ %

14) The price of a pair of shoes increases from $30 to $36. What is the percent increase? ___ %

15) At a coffeeshop, the price of a cup of coffee increased from $1.30 to $1.56. What is the percent increase in the cost of the coffee? _____ %

16) A $40 shirt now selling for $28 is discounted by what percent? _____ %

17) Joe scored 20 out of 25 marks in Algebra, 30 out of 40 marks in science and 68 out of 80 marks in mathematics. In which subject his percentage of marks is best? _____

18) Emma purchased a computer for $408. The computer is regularly priced at $480. What was the percent discount Emma received on the computer? _____

19) A chemical solution contains 12% alcohol. If there is 42 ml of alcohol, what is the volume of the solution? _____

✎ Find the selling price of each item.

20) Original price of a computer: $700

   Tax: 9%, Selling price: $_____

21) Original price of a laptop: $460

   Tax: 20%, Selling price: $_____

22) Nicolas hired a moving company. The company charged $600 for its services, and Nicolas gives the movers a 12% tip. How much does Nicolas tip the movers? $_____

23) Mason has lunch at a restaurant and the cost of his meal is $50. Mason wants to leave a 25% tip. What is Mason's total bill, including tip? $_____

✎ Determine the simple interest for the following loans.

24) $480 at 6% for 5 years. $___

25) $500 at 5% for 3 years. $___

26) $360 at 3.5% for 2 years. $___

27) $600 at 4% for 4 years. $___

✎ Solve.

28) A new car, valued at $25,000, depreciates at 7% per year. What is the value of the car one year after purchase? $_____

29) Sara puts $6,000 into an investment yielding 4% annual simple interest; she left the money in for five years. How much interest does Sara get at the end of those five years? $_____

CHAPTER 5: ANSWERS

1) 12.5%

2) 20%

3) 25%

4) 25%

5) 32%

6) 25%

7) 5%

8) 20%

9) 20%

10) 40%

11) 6.25%

12) 12.5%

13) 25%

14) 20%

15) 20%

16) 30%

17) Mathematics

18) 15%

19) 350

20) $763

21) $552

22) $72

23) $62.50

24) $144

25) $75

26) $25.20

27) $96

28) $23,250

29) $1200

CHAPTER 6:

EXPRESSIONS AND VARIABLES

Math Topics that you'll learn in this chapter:

- ▶ Simplifying Variable Expressions
- ▶ Simplifying Polynomial Expressions
- ▶ The Distributive Property
- ▶ Evaluating One Variable
- ▶ Evaluating Two Variables

SIMPLIFYING VARIABLE EXPRESSIONS

☑ In algebra, a variable is a letter used to stand for a number. The most common letters are $x, y, z, a, b, c, m,$ and n.

☑ An algebraic expression is an expression that contains integers, variables, and math operations such as addition, subtraction, multiplication, division, etc.

☑ In an expression, we can combine "like" terms. (values with same variable and same power)

Examples:

Example 1. Simplify. $(2x + 3x + 4) =$

Solution: In this expression, there are three terms: $2x, 3x,$ and 4. Two terms are "like terms": $2x$ and $3x$. Combine like terms. $2x + 3x = 5x$. Then: $(2x + 3x + 4) = 5x + 4$ (***remember you cannot combine variables and numbers.***)

Example 2. Simplify. $12 - 3x^2 + 5x + 4x^2 =$

Solution: Combine "like" terms: $-3x^2 + 4x^2 = x^2$.
Then: $12 - 3x^2 + 5x + 4x^2 = 12 + x^2 + 5x$. Write in standard form (biggest powers first): $12 + x^2 + 5x = x^2 + 5x + 12$

Example 3. Simplify. $(10x^2 + 2x^2 + 3x) =$

Solution: Combine like terms. Then: $(10x^2 + 2x^2 + 3x) = 12x^2 + 3x$

Example 4. Simplify. $15x - 3x^2 + 9x + 5x^2 =$

Solution: Combine "like" terms: $15x + 9x = 24x$, and $-3x^2 + 5x^2 = 2x^2$
Then: $15x - 3x^2 + 9x + 5x^2 = 24x + 2x^2$. Write in standard form (biggest powers first): $24x + 2x^2 = 2x^2 + 24x$

SIMPLIFYING POLYNOMIAL EXPRESSIONS

☑ In mathematics, a polynomial is an expression consisting of variables and coefficients that involves only the operations of addition, subtraction, multiplication, and non–negative integer exponents of variables.
$$P(x) = a_n x^n + a_{n-1} x^{n-1} + \dots + a_2 x^2 + a_1 x + a_0$$

☑ Polynomials must always be simplified as much as possible. It means you must add together any like terms. (values with same variable and same power)

Examples:

Example 1. Simplify this Polynomial Expressions. $x^2 - 5x^3 + 2x^4 - 4x^3$

Solution: Combine "like" terms: $-5x^3 - 4x^3 = -9x^3$
Then: $x^2 - 5x^3 + 2x^4 - 4x^3 = x^2 - 9x^3 + 2x^4$
Now, write the expression in standard form: $2x^4 - 9x^3 + x^2$

Example 2. Simplify this expression. $(2x^2 - x^3) - (x^3 - 4x^2) =$

Solution: First, use distributive property: multiply $(-)$ into $(x^3 - 4x^2)$
$(2x^2 - x^3) - (x^3 - 4x^2) = 2x^2 - x^3 - x^3 + 4x^2$
Then combine "like" terms: $2x^2 - x^3 - x^3 + 4x^2 = 6x^2 - 2x^3$
And write in standard form: $6x^2 - 2x^3 = -2x^3 + 6x^2$

Example 3. Simplify. $4x^4 - 5x^3 + 15x^4 - 12x^3 =$

Solution: Combine "like" terms:
$-5x^3 - 12x^3 = -17x^3$ and $4x^4 + 15x^4 = 19x^4$
Then: $4x^4 - 5x^3 + 15x^4 - 12x^3 = 19x^4 - 17x^3$

THE DISTRIBUTIVE PROPERTY

☑ The distributive property (or the distributive property of multiplication over addition and subtraction) simplifies and solves expressions in the form of: $a(b + c)$ or $a(b - c)$

☑ The distributive property is multiplying a term outside the parentheses by the terms inside.

☑ Distributive Property rule: $a(b + c) = ab + ac$

Examples:

Example 1. Simply using the distributive property. $(-4)(x - 5)$

Solution: Use Distributive Property rule: $a(b + c) = ab + ac$
$(-4)(x - 5) = (-4 \times x) + (-4) \times (-5) = -4x + 20$

Example 2. Simply. $(3)(2x - 4)$

Solution: Use Distributive Property rule: $a(b + c) = ab + ac$
$(3)(2x - 4) = (3 \times 2x) + (3) \times (-4) = 6x - 12$

Example 3. Simply. $(-3)(3x - 5) + 4x$

Solution: First, simplify $(-3)(3x - 5)$ using the distributive property.
Then: $(-3)(3x - 5) = -9x + 15$
Now combine like terms: $(-3)(3x - 5) + 4x = -9x + 15 + 4x$
In this expression, $-9x$ and $4x$ are "like terms" and we can combine them.
$-9x + 4x = -5x$. Then: $-9x + 15 + 4x = -5x + 15$

EVALUATING ONE VARIABLE

☑ To evaluate one variable expression, find the variable and substitute a number for that variable.

☑ Perform the arithmetic operations.

Examples:

Example 1. Calculate this expression for x = 3. $15 - 3x$

Solution: First, substitute 3 for x
Then: $15 - 3x = 15 - 3(3)$
Now, use order of operation to find the answer: $15 - 3(3) = 15 - 9 = 6$

Example 2. Evaluate this expression for x = 1. $5x - 12$

Solution: First, substitute 1 for x,
Then: $5x - 12 = 5(1) - 12$
Now, use order of operation to find the answer: $5(1) - 12 = 5 - 12 = -7$

Example 3. Find the value of this expression when x = 5. $25 - 4x$

Solution: First, substitute 5 for x,
Then: $25 - 4x = 25 - 4(5) = 25 - 20 = 5$

Example 4. Solve this expression for $x = -2$. $12 + 3x$

Solution: Substitute -2 for x,
Then: $12 + 3x = 12 + 3(-2) = 12 - 6 = 6$

EVALUATING TWO VARIABLES

☑ To evaluate an algebraic expression, substitute a number for each variable.

☑ Perform the arithmetic operations to find the value of the expression.

Examples:

Example 1. Calculate this expression for a $= 3$ and $b = -2$. $3a - 6b$

Solution: First, substitute 3 for a, and -2 for b ,
Then: $3a - 6b = 3(3) - 6(-2)$
Now, use order of operation to find the answer: $3(3) - 6(-2) = 9 + 12 = 21$

Example 2. Evaluate this expression for x $= 3$ and $y = 1$. $3x + 5y$

Solution: Substitute 3 for x, and 1 for y ,
Then: $3x + 5y = 3(3) + 5(1) = 9 + 5 = 14$

Example 3. Find the value of this expression $5(3a - 2b)$ when $a = 1$ and

$b = 2$.

Solution: Substitute 1 for a, and 2 for b ,
Then: $5(3a - 2b) = 15a - 10b = 15(1) - 10(2) = 15 - 20 = -5$

Example 4. Solve this expression. $4x - 3y$, $x = 3$, $y = 5$

Solution: Substitute 3 for x, and 5 for y and simplify.
Then: $4x - 3y = 4(3) - 3(5) = 12 - 15 = -3$

CHAPTER 6: PRACTICES

✎ Simplify each expression.

1) $(9x - 5x - 7 + 4) =$

2) $(-12x - 7x + 6 - 3) =$

3) $(24x - 10x - 3) =$

4) $(-10x + 23x - 6) =$

5) $(32x + 8 - 20x - 4) =$

6) $3 + 6x^2 - 6 =$

7) $3x + 6x^4 - 6x =$

8) $-1 - 2x^2 - 8 =$

9) $67 + 6x - 1 - 9 =$

10) $3x^2 + 9x - 11x - 2 =$

11) $-3x^2 - 5x - 7x + 6 - 7 =$

12) $9x - 2x^2 + 8x =$

13) $12x^2 + 6x - 3x^2 + 12 =$

14) $10x^2 - 8x - 5x^2 + 4 =$

✎ Simplify each polynomial.

15) $8x^2 + 2x^3 - 4x^2 + 10x =$ ⎯⎯⎯⎯⎯⎯⎯⎯⎯⎯⎯⎯⎯⎯⎯

16) $6x^4 + 3x^5 - 9x^4 + 7x^2 =$ ⎯⎯⎯⎯⎯⎯⎯⎯⎯⎯⎯⎯⎯

17) $10x^3 + 12x - 3x^2 - 7x^3 =$ ⎯⎯⎯⎯⎯⎯⎯⎯⎯⎯⎯⎯⎯

18) $(6x^3 - 2x^2) + (4x^2 - 14x) =$ ⎯⎯⎯⎯⎯⎯⎯⎯⎯⎯⎯

19) $(13x^4 + 5x^3) + (2x^3 - 6x^4) =$ ⎯⎯⎯⎯⎯⎯⎯⎯⎯⎯

20) $(14x^5 - 9x^3) - (3x^3 + x^2) =$⎯⎯⎯⎯⎯⎯⎯⎯⎯⎯⎯⎯

21) $(10x^4 + 6x^3) - (x^3 - 65) =$⎯⎯⎯⎯⎯⎯⎯⎯⎯⎯⎯⎯

22) $(26x^4 + 5x^3) - (15x^3 - 3x^4) =$⎯⎯⎯⎯⎯⎯⎯⎯⎯⎯

23) $(10x^2 + 8x^3) + (25x^2 + 4x^3) =$⎯⎯⎯⎯⎯⎯⎯⎯⎯⎯

24) $(8x^4 - 3x^3) + (4x^3 - 7x^4) =$⎯⎯⎯⎯⎯⎯⎯⎯⎯⎯⎯

✎ **Use the distributive property to simply each expression.**

25) $3(6 + 9x) =$ _____

26) $6(4 - 3x) =$ _____

27) $(-8)(3 - 4x) =$ _____

28) $(2 - 5x)(-6) =$ _____

29) $3(7 - 2x) =$ _____

30) $(-x + 1)(-9) =$ _____

31) $(-3)(9x - 5) =$ _____

32) $(2x + 10)6 =$ _____

33) $(-1)(1 - 3x) =$ _____

34) $(6x - 1)(-9) =$ _____

✎ **Evaluate each expression using the value given.**

35) $x = -5$, $14 - x =$ ____

36) $x = -7$, $x + 10 =$ ____

37) $x = 4$, $6x - 8 =$ ____

38) $x = 3$, $9 - 3x =$ ____

39) $x = -8$, $6x - 9 =$ ____

40) $x = 7$, $18 - 3x =$ ____

41) $x = -1$, $14x - 3 =$ ____

42) $x = 5$, $10 - x =$ ____

43) $x = 2$, $28 - 5x =$ ____

44) $x = -9$, $100 - 6x =$ ____

45) $x = 10$, $50 - 8x =$ ____

46) $x = 3$, $61x - 3 =$ ____

47) $x = 3$, $25x - 2 =$ ____

48) $x = -1$, $13 - 4x =$ ____

✎ **Evaluate each expression using the values given.**

49) $x = 2, y = -1$, $3x - 6y =$ _____

50) $a = 3, b = 6$, $7a + 2b =$ _____

51) $x = 3, y = 2$, $5x - 23y + 9 =$ _____

52) $a = 7, b = 5$, $-9a + 3b + 8 =$ _____

53) $x = 3, y = 6$, $3x + 15 + 6y =$ _____

CHAPTER 6: ANSWERS

1) $4x - 3$

2) $-19x + 3$

3) $14x - 3$

4) $13x - 6$

5) $12x + 4$

6) $6x^2 - 3$

7) $6x^4 - 3x$

8) $-2x^2 - 9$

9) $6x + 57$

10) $3x^2 - 2x - 2$

11) $-3x^2 - 12x - 1$

12) $-2x^2 + 17x$

13) $9x^2 + 6x + 12$

14) $5x^2 - 8x + 4$

15) $2x^3 + 4x^2 + 10x$

16) $3x^5 - 3x^4 + 7x^2$

17) $3x^3 - 3x^2 + 12x$

18) $6x^3 + 2x^2 - 14x$

19) $7x^4 + 7x^3$

20) $14x^5 - 12x^3 - x^2$

21) $10x^4 + 5x^3 + 65$

22) $29x^4 - 10x^3$

23) $12x^3 + 35x^2$

24) $x^4 + x^3$

25) $27x + 18$

26) $-18x + 24$

27) $32x - 24$

28) $30x - 12$

29) $-6x + 21$

30) $9x - 9$

31) $-27x + 15$

32) $12x + 60$

33) $3x - 1$

34) $-54x + 9$

35) 19

36) 3

37) 16

38) 0

39) -57

40) -3

41) -17

42) 5

43) 18

44) 154

45) -30

46) 180

47) 73

48) 17

49) 12

50) 33

51) -22

52) -40

53) 60

CHAPTER 7:

EQUATIONS AND INEQUALITIES

Math Topics that you'll learn in this chapter:

- ▶ One-Step Equations
- ▶ Multi-Step Equations
- ▶ System of Equations
- ▶ Graphing Single–Variable Inequalities
- ▶ One-Step Inequalities
- ▶ Multi-Step Inequalities

ONE–STEP EQUATIONS

☑ The values of two expressions on both sides of an equation are equal. Example: $ax = b$. In this equation, ax is equal to b.

☑ Solving an equation means finding the value of the variable.

☑ You only need to perform one Math operation to solve the one-step equations.

☑ To solve a one-step equation, find the inverse (opposite) operation is being performed.

☑ The inverse operations are:

- ❖ Addition and subtraction
- ❖ Multiplication and division

Examples:

Example 1. Solve this equation for x. $3x = 18, x = ?$

Solution: Here, the operation is multiplication (variable x is multiplied by 3) and its inverse operation is division. To solve this equation, divide both sides of equation by 3: $3x = 18 \rightarrow \frac{3x}{3} = \frac{18}{3} \rightarrow x = 6$

Example 2. Solve this equation. $x + 15 = 0$, $x = ?$

Solution: In this equation 15 is added to the variable x. The inverse operation of addition is subtraction. To solve this equation, subtract 15 from both sides of the equation: $x + 15 - 15 = 0 - 15$. Then: $\rightarrow x = -15$

Example 3. Solve this equation for x. $x + 23 = 0$

Solution: Here, the operation is subtraction and its inverse operation is addition. To solve this equation, add 23 to both sides of the equation: $x + 23 - 23 = 0 - 23 \rightarrow x = -23$

MULTI–STEP EQUATIONS

Ø To solve a multi-step equation, combine "like" terms on one side.

Ø Bring variables to one side by adding or subtracting.

Ø Simplify using the inverse of addition or subtraction.

Ø Simplify further by using the inverse of multiplication or division.

Ø Check your solution by plugging the value of the variable into the original equation.

Examples:

Example 1. Solve this equation for x. $3x + 6 = 16 - 2x$

Solution: First, bring variables to one side by adding $2x$ to both sides.
Then: $3x + 6 = 16 - 2x \rightarrow 3x + 6 + 2x = 16 - 2x + 2x$.
Simplify: $5x + 6 = 16$ Now, subtract 6 from both sides of the equation:
$5x + 6 - 6 = 16 - 6 \rightarrow 5x = 10 \rightarrow$ Divide both sides by 5:
$5x = 10 \rightarrow \dfrac{5x}{5} = \dfrac{10}{5} \rightarrow x = 2$

Let's check this solution by substituting the value of 2 for x in the original equation:
$x = 2 \rightarrow 3x + 6 = 16 - 2x \rightarrow 3(2) + 6 = 16 - 2(2) \rightarrow 6 + 6 = 16 - 4 \rightarrow 12 = 12$
The answer $x = 2$ is correct.

Example 2. Solve this equation for x. $-4x + 4 = 16$

Solution: Subtract 4 from both sides of the equation.
$-4x + 4 - 4 = 16 - 4 \rightarrow -4x = 12$
Divide both sides by -4, then: $-4x = 12 \rightarrow \dfrac{-4x}{-4} = \dfrac{12}{-4} \rightarrow x = -3$
Now, check the solution:
$x = -3 \rightarrow -4x + 4 = 16 \rightarrow -4(-3) + 4 = 16 \rightarrow 16 = 16$
The answer $x = -2$ is correct.

SYSTEM OF EQUATIONS

☑ A system of equations contains two equations and two variables. For example, consider the system of equations: $x - y = 1, x + y = 5$

☑ The easiest way to solve a system of equations is using the elimination method. The elimination method uses the addition property of equality. You can add the same value to each side of an equation.

☑ For the first equation above, you can add $x + y$ to the left side and 5 to the right side of the first equation: $x - y + (x + y) = 1 + 5$. Now, if you simplify, you get: $x - y + (x + y) = 1 + 5 \rightarrow 2x = 6 \rightarrow x = 3$. Now, substitute 3 for the x in the first equation: $3 - y = 1$. By solving this equation, $y = 2$

Example:

What is the value of x + y in this system of equations?

$$\begin{cases} x + 2y = 6 \\ 2x - y = -8 \end{cases}$$

Solution: Solving a System of Equations by Elimination:
Multiply the first equation by (-2), then add it to the second equation.

$$\begin{array}{c} -2(x + 2y = 6) \\ \underline{2x - y = -8} \end{array} \Rightarrow \begin{array}{c} -2x - 4y = -12 \\ 2x - y = -8 \end{array} \Rightarrow -5y = -20 \Rightarrow y = 4$$

Plug in the value of y into one of the equations and solve for x.
$x + 2(4) = 6 \Rightarrow x + 8 = 6 \Rightarrow x = 6 - 8 \Rightarrow x = -2$
Thus, $x + y = -2 + 4 = 2$

GRAPHING SINGLE–VARIABLE INEQUALITIES

☑ An inequality compares two expressions using an inequality sign.

☑ Inequality signs are: "less than" <, "greater than" >, "less than or equal to" ≤, and "greater than or equal to" ≥.

☑ To graph a single–variable inequality, find the value of the inequality on the number line.

☑ For less than (<) or greater than (>) draw an open circle on the value of the variable. If there is an equal sign too, then use a filled circle.

☑ Draw an arrow to the right for greater or to the left for less than.

Examples:

Example 1. Draw a graph for this inequality. $x > 3$

Solution: Since the variable is greater than 3, then we need to find 3 in the number line and draw an open circle on it. Then, draw an arrow to the right.

Example 2. Graph this inequality. $x \leq -4$.

Solution: Since the variable is less than or equal to -4, then we need to find -4 in the number line and draw a filled circle on it. Then, draw an arrow to the left.

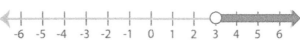

ONE–STEP INEQUALITIES

✓ An inequality compares two expressions using an inequality sign.

✓ Inequality signs are: "less than" <, "greater than" >, "less than or equal to" ≤, and "greater than or equal to" ≥.

✓ You only need to perform one Math operation to solve the one-step inequalities.

✓ To solve one-step inequalities, find the inverse (opposite) operation is being performed.

✓ For dividing or multiplying both sides by negative numbers, flip the direction of the inequality sign.

Examples:

Example 1. Solve this inequality for x. $x + 3 \geq 4$

Solution: The inverse (opposite) operation of addition is subtraction. In this inequality, 3 is added to x. To isolate x we need to subtract 3 from both sides of the inequality.

Then: $x + 3 \geq 4 \rightarrow x + 3 - 3 \geq 4 - 3 \rightarrow x \geq 1$. The solution is: $x \geq 1$

Example 2. Solve the inequality. $x - 5 > -4$.

Solution: 5 is subtracted from x. Add 5 to both sides.
$x - 5 > -4 \rightarrow x - 5 + 5 > -4 + 5 \rightarrow x > 1$

Example 3. Solve. $2x \leq -4$.

Solution: 2 is multiplied to x. Divide both sides by 2.
Then: $2x \leq -4 \rightarrow \frac{2x}{2} \leq \frac{-4}{2} \rightarrow x \leq -2$

Example 4. Solve. $-6x \leq 12$.

Solution: -6 is multiplied to x. Divide both sides by -6. Remember when dividing or multiplying both sides of an inequality by negative numbers, flip the direction of the inequality sign.
Then: $-6x \leq 12 \rightarrow \frac{-6x}{-6} \geq \frac{12}{-6} \rightarrow x \geq -2$

MULTI–STEP INEQUALITIES

☑ To solve a multi-step inequality, combine "like" terms on one side.

☑ Bring variables to one side by adding or subtracting.

☑ Isolate the variable.

☑ Simplify using the inverse of addition or subtraction.

☑ Simplify further by using the inverse of multiplication or division.

☑ For dividing or multiplying both sides by negative numbers, flip the direction of the inequality sign.

Examples:

Example 1. Solve this inequality. $2x - 3 \leq 5$

Solution: In this inequality, 3 is subtracted from $2x$. The inverse of subtraction is addition. Add 3 to both sides of the inequality:

$2x - 3 + 3 \leq 5 + 3 \rightarrow 2x \leq 8$

Now, divide both sides by 2. Then: $2x \leq 8 \rightarrow \frac{2x}{2} \leq \frac{8}{2} \rightarrow x \leq 4$

The solution of this inequality is $x \leq 4$.

Example 2. Solve this inequality. $3x + 9 < 12$

Solution: First, subtract 9 from both sides: $3x + 9 - 9 < 12 - 9$

Then simplify: $3x + 9 - 9 < 12 - 9 \rightarrow 3x < 3$

Now divide both sides by 3: $\frac{3x}{3} < \frac{3}{3} \rightarrow x < 1$

Example 3. Solve this inequality. $-2x + 4 \geq 6$

Solution: First, subtract 4 from both sides:

$-2x + 4 - 4 \geq 6 - 4 \rightarrow -2x \geq 2$

Divide both sides by -2. Remember that you need to flip the direction of inequality sign. $-2x \geq 2 \rightarrow \frac{-2x}{-2} \leq \frac{2}{-2} \rightarrow x \leq -1$

CHAPTER 7: PRACTICES

✍ Solve each equation. (One–Step Equations)

1) $x + 8 = 4, x =$ _____

2) $3 = 12 - x, x =$ _____

3) $-4 = 9 + x, x =$ _____

4) $x - 6 = -9, x =$ _____

5) $18 = x + 8, x =$ _____

6) $15 - x = -4, x =$ _____

7) $25 - x = 8, x =$ _____

8) $6 + x = 27, x =$ _____

9) $10 - x = -8, x =$ _____

10) $36 - x = -5, x =$ _____

✍ Solve each equation. (Multi–Step Equations)

11) $6(x + 8) = 24, \ x =$ ____

12) $-9(9 - x) = 18, x =$ ____

13) $7 = -7 (x + 3), x =$ ____

14) $-16 = 2(10 - 6x), x =$ ____

15) $6(x + 1) = -24, x =$ ____

16) $-3(7 + 9x) = 33, x =$ ____

17) $-7(5 - x) = 14, x =$ ____

18) $-1(3 - x) = 10, x =$ ____

✍ Solve each system of equations.

19) $\begin{cases} -2x + 2y = -4 \\ 4x - 9y = 28 \end{cases}$ $x =$ \
$y =$

20) $\begin{cases} x + 8y = -5 \\ 2x + 6y = 0 \end{cases}$ $x =$ \
$y =$

21) $\begin{cases} 4x - 3y = -2 \\ x - y = 3 \end{cases}$ $x =$ \
$y =$

22) $\begin{cases} 2x + 9y = 17 \\ -3x + 8y = 39 \end{cases}$ $x =$ \
$y =$

✍ **Draw a graph for each inequality.**

23) $x \leq -3$

24) $x > -5$

✍ **Solve each inequality and graph it.**

25) $x - 2 \geq -2$

26) $2x - 3 < 9$

✍ **Solve each inequality.**

27) $4x + 12 > -8$

28) $3x + 14 > 5$

29) $-16 + 3x \leq 20$

30) $-18 + 6x \leq -24$

31) $8 + 2x \leq 16$

32) $5(x + 2) \geq 6$

33) $2(3 + x) \geq 10$

34) $6x - 10 < 14$

35) $12x + 8 < 32$

36) $8(4 + x) \geq 16$

37) $2(x - 5) \geq 18$

38) $x + 10 < 3$

39) $2(x - 4) \geq 20$

40) $-8 + 9x > 28$

41) $-4 + 8x > 60$

42) $-2 + 7x > 40$

CHAPTER 7: ANSWERS

1) -4

2) 9

3) -13

4) -3

5) 10

6) 19

7) 17

8) 21

9) 18

10) 41

11) -4

12) 11

13) -4

14) 3

15) -5

16) -2

17) 7

18) 13

19) $x = -2, y = -4$

20) $x = 3, y = -1$

21) $x = -11, y = -14$

22) $x = -5, y = 3$

23) $x \leq -3$

24) $x > -5$

25) $x \geq 0$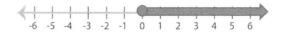

26) $x < 6$

27) $x > -5$

28) $x > -3$

29) $x \leq 12$

30) $x \leq -1$

31) $x \leq 4$

32) $x \geq -\frac{4}{5}$

33) $x \geq 2$

34) $x < 4$

35) $x < 2$

36) $x \geq -2$

37) $x \geq 14$

38) $x < -7$

39) $x \geq 14$

40) $x > 4$

41) $x > 8$

42) $x > 6$

CHAPTER 8:

LINES AND SLOPE

Math Topics that you'll learn in this chapter:

▶ Finding Slope

▶ Graphing Lines Using Slope–Intercept Form

▶ Writing Linear Equations

▶ Graphing Linear Inequalities

▶ Finding Midpoint

▶ Finding Distance of Two Points

FINDING SLOPE

☑ The slope of a line represents the direction of a line on the coordinate plane.

☑ A coordinate plane contains two perpendicular number lines. The horizontal line is x and the vertical line is y. The point at which the two axes intersect is called the origin. An ordered pair (x, y) shows the location of a point.

☑ A line on a coordinate plane can be drawn by connecting two points.

☑ To find the slope of a line, we need the equation of the line or two points on the line.

☑ The slope of a line with two points A (x_1, y_1) and B (x_2, y_2) can be found by using this formula: $\frac{y_2 - y_1}{x_2 - x_1} = \frac{rise}{run}$

☑ The equation of a line is typically written as $y = mx + b$ where m is the slope and b is the y-intercept.

Examples:

Example 1. Find the slope of the line through these two points:

A$(2, -7)$ and $B(4, 3)$.

Solution: Slope $= \frac{y_2 - y_1}{x_2 - x_1}$. Let (x_1, y_1) be $A(2, -7)$ and (x_2, y_2) be $B(4, 3)$.
(Remember, you can choose any point for (x_1, y_1) and (x_2, y_2)).
Then: slope $= \frac{y_2 - y_1}{x_2 - x_1} = \frac{3 - (-7)}{4 - 2} = \frac{10}{2} = 5$

The slope of the line through these two points is 5.

Example 2. Find the slope of the line with equation $y = 3x + 6$

Solution: when the equation of a line is written in the form of $y = mx + b$, the slope is m. In this line: $y = 3x + 6$, the slope is 3.

GRAPHING LINES USING SLOPE–INTERCEPT FORM

☑ Slope–intercept form of a line: given the slope m and the y–intercept (the intersection of the line and y-axis) b, then the equation of the line is:

$$y = mx + b$$

☑ To draw the graph of a linear equation in a slope-intercept form on the xy coordinate plane, find two points on the line by plugging two values for x and calculating the values of y.

☑ You can also use the slope (m) and one point to graph the line.

Example:

Example 1. Sketch the graph of $y = 2x - 4$.

Solution: To graph this line, we need to find two points. When x is zero the value of y is -4. And when x is 2 the value of y is 0.

$$x = 0 \rightarrow y = 2(0) - 4 = -4,$$
$$y = 0 \rightarrow 0 = 2x - 4 \rightarrow x = 2$$

Now, we have two points:
$(0, -4)$ and $(2, 0)$.
Find the points on the coordinate plane and graph the line. Remember that the slope of the line is 2.

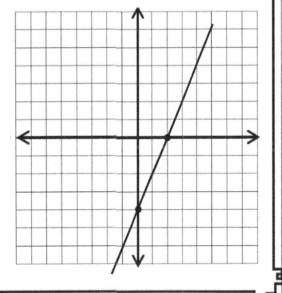

WRITING LINEAR EQUATIONS

☑ The equation of a line in slope-intercept form: $y = mx + b$

☑ To write the equation of a line, first identify the slope.

☑ Find the y-intercept. This can be done by substituting the slope and the coordinates of a point (x, y) on the line.

Examples:

Example 1. What is the equation of the line that passes through $(2, -4)$ and has a slope of 8?

Solution: The general slope-intercept form of the equation of a line is $y = mx + b$, where m is the slope and b is the y-intercept.
By substitution of the given point and given slope:
$y = mx + b \rightarrow -4 = (2)(8) + b$. So, $b = -4 - 16 = -20$, and the required equation is $y = 8x - 20$

Example 2. Write the equation of the line through two points $A(2, 1)$ and $B(-2, 5)$.

Solution: First, find the slope: $Slop = \frac{y_2 - y_1}{x_2 - x_1} = \frac{5 - 1}{-2 - 2} = \frac{4}{-4} = -1 \rightarrow m = -1$
To find the value of b, use either points and plug in the values of x and y in the equation. The answer will be the same: $y = -x + b$. Let's check both points. Then: $(2, 1) \rightarrow y = mx + b \rightarrow 1 = -1(2) + b \rightarrow b = 3$
$(-2, 5) \rightarrow y = mx + b \rightarrow 5 = -1(-2) + b \rightarrow b = 3$.
The y-intercept of the line is 3. The equation of the line is: $y = -x + 3$

Example 3. What is the equation of the line that passes through $(2, -1)$ and has a slope of 5?

Solution: The general slope-intercept form of the equation of a line is $y = mx + b$, where m is the slope and b is the y-intercept. By substitution of the given point and given slope:$y = mx + b \rightarrow -1 = (5)(2) + b$
So, $b = -1 - 10 = -11$, and the equation of the line is: $y = 5x - 11$.

FINDING MIDPOINT

☑ The middle of a line segment is its midpoint.

☑ The Midpoint of two endpoints A (x_1, y_1) and B (x_2, y_2) can be found using this formula: $M\left(\frac{x_1+x_2}{2}, \frac{y_1+y_2}{2}\right)$

Examples:

Example 1. Find the midpoint of the line segment with the given endpoints. $(1, -3), (3, 7)$

Solution: Midpoint $= \left(\frac{x_1+x_2}{2}, \frac{y_1+y_2}{2}\right) \rightarrow (x_1, y_1) = (1, -3)$ and $(x_2, y_2) = (3, 7)$

Midpoint $= \left(\frac{1+3}{2}, \frac{-3+7}{2}\right) \rightarrow \left(\frac{4}{2}, \frac{4}{2}\right) \rightarrow M(2, 2)$

Example 2. Find the midpoint of the line segment with the given endpoints. $(-4, 5), (8, -7)$

Solution: Midpoint $= \left(\frac{x_1+x_2}{2}, \frac{y_1+y_2}{2}\right) \rightarrow (x_1, y_1) = (-4, 5)$ and $(x_2, y_2) = (8, -7)$

Midpoint $= \left(\frac{-4+8}{2}, \frac{5-7}{2}\right) \rightarrow \left(\frac{4}{2}, \frac{-2}{2}\right) \rightarrow M(2, -1)$

Example 3. Find the midpoint of the line segment with the given endpoints. $(5, -2), (1, 10)$

Solution: Midpoint $= \left(\frac{x_1+x_2}{2}, \frac{y_1+y_2}{2}\right) \rightarrow (x_1, y_1) = (5, -2)$ and $(x_2, y_2) = (1, 10)$

Midpoint $= \left(\frac{5+1}{2}, \frac{-2+10}{2}\right) \rightarrow \left(\frac{6}{2}, \frac{8}{2}\right) \rightarrow M(3, 4)$

Example 4. Find the midpoint of the line segment with the given endpoints. $(2, 3), (12, -9)$

Solution: Midpoint $= \left(\frac{x_1+x_2}{2}, \frac{y_1+y_2}{2}\right) \rightarrow (x_1, y_1) = (2, 3)$ and $(x_2, y_2) = (12, -3)$

Midpoint $= \left(\frac{2+12}{2}, \frac{3-9}{2}\right) \rightarrow \left(\frac{14}{2}, \frac{-6}{2}\right) \rightarrow M(7, -3)$

FINDING DISTANCE OF TWO POINTS

☑ Use the following formula to find the distance of two points with the coordinates A (x_1, y_1) and B (x_2, y_2):

$$d = \sqrt{(x_2 - x_1)^2 + (y_2 - y_1)^2}$$

Examples:

Example 1. Find the distance between $(4, 6)$ and $(1, 2)$.

 Solution: Use distance of two points formula: $d = \sqrt{(x_2 - x_1)^2 + (y_2 - y_1)^2}$ $(x_1, y_1) = (4, 6)$ and $(x_2, y_2) = (1, 2)$. Then: $d = \sqrt{(x_2 - x_1)^2 + (y_2 - y_1)^2} \rightarrow$
$d = \sqrt{\left(1 - (4)\right)^2 + (2 - 6)^2} = \sqrt{(-3)^2 + (-4)^2} = \sqrt{9 + 16} = \sqrt{25} = 5 \rightarrow d = 5$

Example 2. Find the distance of two points $(-6, -10)$ and $(-2, -10)$.

Solution: Use distance of two points formula: $d = \sqrt{(x_2 - x_1)^2 + (y_2 - y_1)^2}$
$(x_1, y_1) = (-6, -10)$, and $(x_2, y_2) = (-2, -10)$
Then: $d = \sqrt{(x_2 - x_1)^2 + (y_2 - y_1)^2} \rightarrow d = \sqrt{(-2 - (-6))^2 + \left(-10 - (-10)\right)^2} =$
$\sqrt{(4)^2 + (0)^2} = \sqrt{16 + 0} = \sqrt{16} = 4$. Then: $d = 4$

Example 3. Find the distance between $(-6, 5)$ and $(-2, 2)$.

 Solution: Use distance of two points formula: $d = \sqrt{(x_2 - x_1)^2 + (y_2 - y_1)^2}$
$(x_1, y_1) = (-6, 5)$ and $(x_2, y_2) = (-2, 2)$. Then: $d = \sqrt{(x_2 - x_1)^2 + (y_2 - y_1)^2}$
$d = \sqrt{\left(-2 - (-6)\right)^2 + (2 - 5)^2} = \sqrt{(4)^2 + (-3)^2} = \sqrt{16 + 9} = \sqrt{25} = 5$

GRAPHING LINEAR INEQUALITIES

- To graph a linear inequality, first draw a graph of the "equals" line.

- Use a dash line for less than ($<$) and greater than ($>$) signs and a solid line for less than and equal to ($\leq$) and greater than and equal to ($\geq$).

- Choose a testing point. (it can be any point on both sides of the line.)

- Put the value of (x, y) of that point in the inequality. If that works, that part of the line is the solution. If the values don't work, then the other part of the line is the solution.

Example:

Sketch the graph of inequality: $y < 2x + 4$

Solution: To draw the graph of $y < 2x + 4$, you first need to graph the line: $y = 2x + 4$

Since there is a less than ($<$) sign, draw a dash line.

The slope is 2 and y-intercept is 4.

Then, choose a testing point and substitute the value of x and y from that point into the inequality. The easiest point to test is the origin: $(0, 0)$

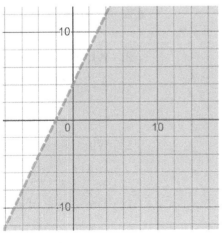

$$(0,0) \rightarrow y < 2x + 4 \rightarrow 0 < 2(0) + 4 \rightarrow 0 < 4$$

This is correct! 0 is less than 4. So, this part of the line (on the right side) is the solution of this inequality.

CHAPTER 8: PRACTICES

✎ Find the slope of each line.

1) $y = x - 3$

2) $y = -6x + 4$

3) $y = 3x - 9$

4) Line through $(-1, 3)$ and $(5, 0)$

5) Line through $(4, 0)$ and $(-2, 6)$

6) Line through $(-3, -6)$ and $(0, 3)$

✎ Sketch the graph of each line. (Using Slope–Intercept Form)

7) $y = x + 4$

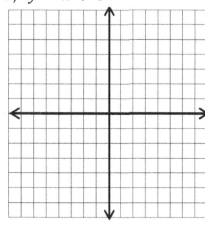

8) $y = 2x - 5$

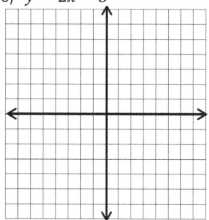

✎ Solve.

9) What is the equation of a line with slope 3 and intercept 18? _____

10) What is the equation of a line with slope 2 and passes through point $(2, 6)$?

_____

11) What is the equation of a line with slope -4 and passes through point $(-4, 8)$?

_____

12) The slope of a line is -2 and it passes through point $(-4, 3)$. What is the equation of the line? _____

13) The slope of a line is 5 and it passes through point $(-6, 3)$. What is the equation of the line? _____

✍ **Sketch the graph of each linear inequality.**

14) $y > 2x - 2$

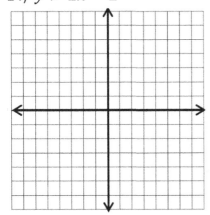

15) $y < -x + 3$

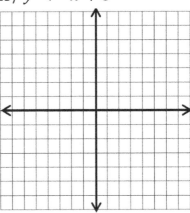

✍ **Find the midpoint of the line segment with the given endpoints.**

16) $(3, 6), (-1, 8)$

17) $(-2, 4), (8, 4)$

18) $(8, -3), (-2, 1)$

19) $(15, -9), (-3, 1)$

20) $(-10, 4), (6, 8)$

21) $(6, 12), (2, -4)$

22) $(4, 8), (-2, 0)$

23) $(0, 8), (-6, 6)$

✍ **Find the distance between each pair of points.**

24) $(-1, 6), (-5, 3)$

25) $(2, -2), (7, 10)$

26) $(-1, -4), (5, 4)$

27) $(6, -1), (-6, 8)$

28) $(2, -5), (-6, 10)$

29) $(0, 6), (4, 6)$

30) $(6, 3), (9, -1)$

31) $(0, -2), (10, 22)$

32) $(5, -6), (-11, 24)$

33) $(6, -10), (-6, 6)$

CHAPTER 8: ANSWERS

1) 1

3) 3

5) −1

2) −6

4) $-\frac{1}{2}$

6) 3

7) $y = x + 4$

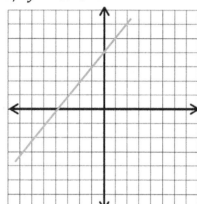

8) $y = 2x - 5$

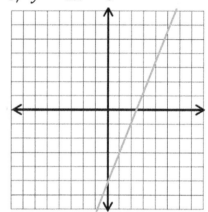

9) $y = 3x + 18$

11) $y = -4x - 8$

13) $y = 5x + 33$

10) $y = 2x + 2$

12) $y = -2x - 5$

14) $y > 2x - 2$

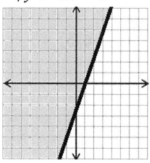

15) $y < -x + 3$

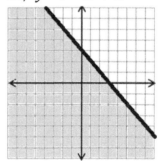

16) $(1, 7)$

22) $(1, 4)$

28) 17

17) $(3, 4)$

23) $(-3, 7)$

29) 4

18) $(3, -1)$

24) 5

30) 5

19) $(6, -4)$

25) 13

31) 26

20) $(-2, 6)$

26) 10

32) 34

21) $(4, 4)$

27) 15

33) 20

CHAPTER 9:

EXPONENTS AND VARIABLES

Math Topics that you'll learn in this chapter:

▶ Multiplication Property of Exponents

▶ Division Property of Exponents

▶ Powers of Products and Quotients

▶ Zero and Negative Exponents

▶ Negative Exponents and Negative Bases

▶ Scientific Notation

▶ Radicals

MULTIPLICATION PROPERTY OF EXPONENTS

☑ Exponents are shorthand for repeated multiplication of the same number by itself. For example, instead of 2×2, we can write 2^2. For $3 \times 3 \times 3 \times 3$, we can write 3^4

☑ In algebra, a variable is a letter used to stand for a number. The most common letters are: $x, y, z, a, b, c, m,$ and n.

☑ Exponent's rules: $x^a \times x^b = x^{a+b}$, $\frac{x^a}{x^b} = x^{a-b}$

$$(x^a)^b = x^{a \times b} \qquad\qquad (xy)^a = x^a \times y^a \qquad\qquad \left(\frac{a}{b}\right)^c = \frac{a^c}{b^c}$$

Examples:

Example 1. Multiply. $4x^3 \times 2x^2$

Solution: Use Exponent's rules: $x^a \times x^b = x^{a+b} \rightarrow x^3 \times x^2 = x^{3+2} = x^5$
Then: $4x^3 \times 2x^2 = 8x^5$

Example 2. Simplify. $\left(x^3 y^5\right)^2$

Solution: Use Exponent's rules: $(x^a)^b = x^{a \times b}$.
Then: $\left(x^3 y^5\right)^2 = x^{3 \times 2} y^{5 \times 2} = x^6 y^{10}$

Example 3. Multiply. $-2x^5 \times 7x^3$

Solution: Use Exponent's rules: $x^a \times x^b = x^{a+b} \rightarrow x^5 \times x^3 = x^{5+3} = x^8$
Then: $-2x^5 \times 7x^3 = -14x^8$

Example 4. Simplify. $(x^2 y^4)^3$

Solution: Use Exponent's rules: $(x^a)^b = x^{a \times b}$.
Then: $(x^2 y^4)^3 = x^{2 \times 3} y^{4 \times 3} = x^6 y^{12}$

DIVISION PROPERTY OF EXPONENTS

☑ Exponents are shorthand for repeated multiplication of the same number by itself. For example, instead of 3×3, we can write 3^2. For $2 \times 2 \times 2$, we can write 2^3

☑ For division of exponents use following formulas:

$$\frac{x^a}{x^b} = x^{a-b} , x \neq 0, \quad \frac{x^a}{x^b} = \frac{1}{x^{b-a}} , x \neq 0, \qquad \frac{1}{x^b} = x^{-b}$$

Examples:

Example 1. Simplify. $\frac{12x^2y}{4xy^3} =$

Solution: First, cancel the common factor: $4 \to \frac{12x^2y}{4xy^3} = \frac{3x^2y}{xy^3}$

Use Exponent's rules: $\frac{x^a}{x^b} = x^{a-b} \to \frac{x^2}{x} = x^{2-1} = x$ and $\frac{y}{y^3} = \frac{1}{y^{3-1}} = \frac{1}{y^2}$

Then: $\frac{12x^2y}{4xy^3} = \frac{3x}{y^2}$

Example 2. Simplify. $\frac{18x^6}{2x^3} =$

Solution: Use Exponent's rules: $\frac{x^a}{x^b} = x^{a-b} \to \frac{x^6}{x^3} = x^{6-3} = x^3$

Then: $\frac{18x^6}{2x^3} = 9x^3$

Example 3. Simplify. $\frac{8x^3y}{40x^2y^3} =$

Solution: First, cancel the common factor: $8 \to \frac{8x^3y}{40x^2y^3} = \frac{x^3y}{5x^2y^3}$

Use Exponent's rules: $\frac{x^a}{x^b} = x^{a-b} \to \frac{x^3}{x^2} = x^{3-2} = x$

Then: $\frac{8x^3y}{40x^2y^3} = \frac{xy}{5y^3} \to$ now cancel the common factor: $y \to \frac{xy}{5y^3} = \frac{x}{5y^2}$

POWERS OF PRODUCTS AND QUOTIENTS

☑ Exponents are shorthand for repeated multiplication of the same number by itself. For example, instead of $2 \times 2 \times 2$, we can write 2^3. For $3 \times 3 \times 3 \times 3$, we can write 3^4

☑ For any nonzero numbers a and b and any integer x, $(ab)^x = a^x \times b^x$ and $\left(\frac{a}{b}\right)^c = \frac{a^c}{b^c}$

Examples:

Example 1. Simplify. $(6x^2y^4)^2$

Solution: Use Exponent's rules: $(x^a)^b = x^{a \times b}$
$(6x^2y^4)^2 = (6)^2(x^2)^2(y^4)^2 = 36x^{2 \times 2}y^{4 \times 2} = 36x^4y^8$

Example 2. Simplify. $\left(\frac{5x}{2x^2}\right)^2$

Solution: First, cancel the common factor: $x \rightarrow \left(\frac{5x}{2x^2}\right)^2 = \left(\frac{5}{2x}\right)^2$
Use Exponent's rules: $\left(\frac{a}{b}\right)^c = \frac{a^c}{b^c}$, Then: $\left(\frac{5}{2x}\right)^2 = \frac{5^2}{(2x)^2} = \frac{25}{4x^2}$

Example 3. Simplify. $\left(3x^5y^4\right)^2$

Solution: Use Exponent's rules: $(x^a)^b = x^{a \times b}$
$\left(3x^5y^4\right)^2 = (3)^2\left(x^5\right)^2(y^4)^2 = 9x^{5 \times 2}y^{4 \times 2} = 9x^{10}y^8$

Example 4. Simplify. $\left(\frac{2x}{3x^2}\right)^2$

Solution: First, cancel the common factor: $x \rightarrow \left(\frac{2x}{3x^2}\right)^2 = \left(\frac{2}{3x}\right)^2$
Use Exponent's rules: $\left(\frac{a}{b}\right)^c = \frac{a^c}{b^c}$, Then: $\left(\frac{2}{3x}\right)^2 = \frac{2^2}{(3x)^2} = \frac{4}{9x^2}$

ZERO AND NEGATIVE EXPONENTS

✅ Zero-Exponent Rule: $a^0 = 1$, this means that anything raised to the zero power is 1. For example: $(5xy)^0 = 1$

✅ A negative exponent simply means that the base is on the wrong side of the fraction line, so you need to flip the base to the other side. For instance, "x^{-2}" (pronounced as "ecks to the minus two") just means "x^2" but underneath, as in $\frac{1}{x^2}$.

Examples:

Example 1. Evaluate. $\left(\frac{2}{3}\right)^{-2} =$

Solution: Use negative exponent's rule: $\left(\frac{x^a}{x^b}\right)^{-2} = \left(\frac{x^b}{x^a}\right)^2 \rightarrow \left(\frac{2}{3}\right)^{-2} = \left(\frac{3}{2}\right)^2 =$
Then: $\left(\frac{3}{2}\right)^2 = \frac{3^2}{2^2} = \frac{9}{4}$

Example 2. Evaluate. $\left(\frac{4}{5}\right)^{-3} =$

Solution: Use negative exponent's rule: $\left(\frac{x^a}{x^b}\right)^{-2} = \left(\frac{x^b}{x^a}\right)^2 \rightarrow \left(\frac{4}{5}\right)^{-3} = \left(\frac{5}{4}\right)^3 =$
Then: $\left(\frac{5}{4}\right)^3 = \frac{5^3}{4^3} = \frac{125}{64}$

Example 3. Evaluate. $\left(\frac{x}{y}\right)^0 =$

Solution: Use zero-exponent Rule: $a^0 = 1$
Then: $\left(\frac{x}{y}\right)^0 = 1$

Example 4. Evaluate. $\left(\frac{5}{6}\right)^{-1} =$

Solution: Use negative exponent's rule: $\left(\frac{x^a}{x^b}\right)^{-2} = \left(\frac{x^b}{x^a}\right)^2 \rightarrow \left(\frac{5}{6}\right)^{-1} = \left(\frac{6}{5}\right)^1 = \frac{6}{5}$

NEGATIVE EXPONENTS AND NEGATIVE BASES

☑ A negative exponent is the reciprocal of that number with a positive exponent. $(3)^{-2} = \frac{1}{3^2}$

☑ To simplify a negative exponent, make the power positive!

☑ The parenthesis is important! -5^{-2} is not the same as $(-5)^{-2}$

$$-5^{-2} = -\frac{1}{5^2} \text{ and } (-5)^{-2} = +\frac{1}{5^2}$$

Examples:

Example 1. Simplify. $\left(\frac{5a}{6c}\right)^{-2} =$

Solution: Use negative exponent's rule: $\left(\frac{x^a}{x^b}\right)^{-2} = \left(\frac{x^b}{x^a}\right)^2 \rightarrow \left(\frac{5a}{6c}\right)^{-2} = \left(\frac{6c}{5a}\right)^2$

Now use exponent's rule: $\left(\frac{a}{b}\right)^c = \frac{a^c}{b^c} \rightarrow = \left(\frac{6c}{5a}\right)^2 = \frac{6^2c^2}{5^2a^2}$

Then: $\frac{6^2c^2}{5^2a^2} = \frac{36c^2}{25a^2}$

Example 2. Simplify. $\left(\frac{2x}{3yz}\right)^{-3} =$

Solution: Use negative exponent's rule: $\left(\frac{x^a}{x^b}\right)^{-2} = \left(\frac{x^b}{x^a}\right)^2 \rightarrow \left(\frac{2x}{3yz}\right)^{-3} = \left(\frac{3yz}{2x}\right)^3$

Now use exponent's rule: $\left(\frac{a}{b}\right)^c = \frac{a^c}{b^c} \rightarrow \left(\frac{3yz}{2x}\right)^3 = \frac{3^3y^3z^3}{2^3x^3} = \frac{27y^3z^3}{8x^3}$

Example 3. Simplify. $\left(\frac{3a}{2c}\right)^{-2} =$

Solution: Use negative exponent's rule: $\left(\frac{x^a}{x^b}\right)^{-2} = \left(\frac{x^b}{x^a}\right)^2 \rightarrow \left(\frac{3a}{2c}\right)^{-2} = \left(\frac{2c}{3a}\right)^2$

Now use exponent's rule: $\left(\frac{a}{b}\right)^c = \frac{a^c}{b^c} \rightarrow = \left(\frac{2c}{3a}\right)^2 = \frac{2^2c^2}{3^2a^2}$

Then: $\frac{2^2c^2}{3^2a^2} = \frac{4c^2}{9a^2}$

SCIENTIFIC NOTATION

- ☑ Scientific notation is used to write very big or very small numbers in decimal form.

- ☑ In scientific notation, all numbers are written in the form of: $m \times 10^n$, where m is greater than 1 and less than 10.

- ☑ To convert a number from scientific notation to standard form, move the decimal point to the left (if the exponent of ten is a negative number), or to the right (if the exponent is positive).

Examples:

Example 1. Write 0.00015 in scientific notation.

Solution: First, move the decimal point to the right so you have a number between 1 and 10. That number is 1.5. Now, determine how many places the decimal moved in step 1 by the power of 10. We moved the decimal point 4 digits to the right. Then: $10^{-4} \rightarrow$ When the decimal moved to the right, the exponent is negative. Then: $0.00015 = 1.5 \times 10^{-4}$

Example 2. Write 9.5×10^{-5} in standard notation.

Solution: $10^{-5} \rightarrow$ When the decimal moved to the right, the exponent is negative. Then: $9.5 \times 10^{-5} = 0.000095$

Example 3. Write 0.00012 in scientific notation.

Solution: First, move the decimal point to the right so you have a number between 1 and 10. Then: $m = 1.2$, Now, determine how many places the decimal moved in step 1 by the power of 10.
$10^{-4} \rightarrow$ Then: $0.00012 = 1.2 \times 10^{-4}$

Example 4. Write 8.3×10^5 in standard notation.
Solution: $10^{-5} \rightarrow$ The exponent is positive 5. Then, move the decimal point to the right five digits. (remember 8.3 = 8.30000),
Then: $8.3 \times 10^5 = 830,000$

RADICALS

✓ If n is a positive integer and x is a real number, then: $\sqrt[n]{x} = x^{\frac{1}{n}}$,

$$\sqrt[n]{xy} = x^{\frac{1}{n}} \times y^{\frac{1}{n}}, \ \sqrt[n]{\frac{x}{y}} = \frac{x^{\frac{1}{n}}}{y^{\frac{1}{n}}}, \text{ and } \sqrt[n]{x} \times \sqrt[n]{y} = \sqrt[n]{xy}$$

✓ A square root of x is a number r whose square is: $r^2 = x$ (r is a square root of x)

✓ To add and subtract radicals, we need to have the same values under the radical. For example: $\sqrt{3} + \sqrt{3} = 2\sqrt{3}$, $3\sqrt{5} - \sqrt{5} = 2\sqrt{5}$

Examples:

Example 1. Find the square root of $\sqrt{169}$.

Solution: First, factor the number: $169 = 13^2$, Then: $\sqrt{169} = \sqrt{13^2}$,
Now use radical rule: $\sqrt[n]{a^n} = a$. Then: $\sqrt{169} = \sqrt{13^2} = 13$

Example 2. Evaluate. $\sqrt{9} \times \sqrt{25} =$

Solution: Find the values of $\sqrt{9}$ and $\sqrt{25}$. Then: $\sqrt{9} \times \sqrt{25} = 3 \times 5 = 15$

Example 3. Solve. $7\sqrt{2} + 4\sqrt{2}$.

Solution: Since we have the same values under the radical, we can add these two radicals: $7\sqrt{2} + 4\sqrt{2} = 11\sqrt{2}$

Example 4. Evaluate. $\sqrt{2} \times \sqrt{8} =$

Solution: Use this radical rule: $\sqrt[n]{x} \times \sqrt[n]{y} = \sqrt[n]{xy} \rightarrow \sqrt{2} \times \sqrt{8} = \sqrt{16}$
The square root of 16 is 4. Then: $\sqrt{2} \times \sqrt{8} = \sqrt{16} = 4$

CHAPTER 9: PRACTICES

✎ Find the products.

1) $2x^3 \times 4xy^2 =$

2) $6x^2y \times 8x^2y^2 =$

3) $5x^3y^2 \times 3x^2y^3 =$

4) $7xy^4 \times 4x^2y =$

5) $3x^4y^5 \times 9x^3y^2 =$

6) $6x^3y^2 \times 7x^3y^3 =$

7) $4x^3y^6 \times 2x^4y^2 =$

8) $7x^4y^3 \times 3x^3y^2 =$

9) $10x^5y^2 \times 10x^4y^3 =$

10) $8x^2y^3 \times 5x^6y^2 =$

11) $9y^5 \times 2x^6y^3 =$

12) $7x^4 \times 7x^2y^2 =$

✎ Simplify.

13) $\dfrac{3^3 \times 3^4}{3^9 \times 3} =$

14) $\dfrac{6x}{30x^2} =$

15) $\dfrac{18x^4}{6x^3} =$

16) $\dfrac{42x^3}{56x^3y^2} =$

17) $\dfrac{18y^3}{54x^4y^4} =$

18) $\dfrac{150x^3y^5}{50x^2y^3} =$

19) $\dfrac{2^3 \times 2^2}{7^2 \times 7} =$

20) $\dfrac{12x}{2x^2} =$

21) $\dfrac{25x^6}{5x^3} =$

22) $\dfrac{48y^4}{56x^5y^3} =$

✎ Solve.

23) $(3x^2y^6)^3 =$

24) $(2x^3y^4)^5 =$

25) $(2x \times 5xy^2)^2 =$

26) $(3x \times 2y^3)^2 =$

27) $\left(\dfrac{8x}{x^3}\right)^3 =$

28) $\left(\dfrac{9y}{3y^2}\right)^3 =$

29) $\left(\dfrac{6x^3y^4}{2x^4y^2}\right)^3 =$

30) $\left(\dfrac{27x^4y^4}{54x^3y^5}\right)^2 =$

31) $\left(\dfrac{9x^8y^4}{3x^5y^2}\right)^2 =$

32) $\left(\dfrac{35x^7y^4}{7x^5y^3}\right)^2 =$

✍ Evaluate each expression. (Zero and Negative Exponents)

33) $\left(\frac{1}{8}\right)^{-3} =$

34) $\left(\frac{1}{6}\right)^{-2} =$

35) $\left(\frac{3}{4}\right)^{-2} =$

36) $\left(\frac{4}{9}\right)^{-2} =$

37) $\left(\frac{1}{4}\right)^{-4} =$

38) $\left(\frac{2}{7}\right)^{-3} =$

✍ Write each expression with positive exponents.

39) $18x^{-2}y^{-6} =$

40) $35x^{-3}y^{-5} =$

41) $-12y^{-4} =$

42) $-25x^{-6} =$

43) $15a^{-3}b^6 =$

44) $20a^6b^{-5}c^{-3} =$

45) $46x^6y^{-3}z^{-7} =$

46) $\frac{16y}{x^3y^{-3}} =$

47) $\frac{24a^{-3}b}{-16c^{-3}}$

✍ Write each number in scientific notation.

48) $0.00521 =$

49) $0.000067 =$

50) $25,000 =$

51) $36,000,000 =$

✍ Evaluate.

52) $\sqrt{6} \times \sqrt{6} =$ ....

53) $\sqrt{49} - \sqrt{4} =$ ....

54) $\sqrt{36} + \sqrt{64} =$ ....

55) $\sqrt{9} \times \sqrt{49} =$ ....

56) $\sqrt{2} \times \sqrt{18} =$ ....

57) $3\sqrt{5} + 2\sqrt{5} =$ ....

CHAPTER 9: ANSWERS

1) $8x^4y^2$

2) $48x^4y^3$

3) $15x^5y^5$

4) $28x^3y^5$

5) $27x^7y^7$

6) $42x^6y^5$

7) $8x^7y^8$

8) $21x^7y^5$

9) $100x^9y^5$

10) $40x^8y^5$

11) $18x^6y^8$

12) $49x^6y^2$

13) $\frac{1}{27}$

14) $\frac{1}{5x}$

15) $3x$

16) $\frac{3}{4y^2}$

17) $\frac{1}{3x^4y}$

18) $3xy^2$

19) $\frac{32}{343}$

20) $\frac{6}{x}$

21) $5x^3$

22) $\frac{6y}{7x^5}$

23) $27x^6y^{18}$

24) $32x^{15}y^{20}$

25) $100x^4y^4$

26) $36x^2y^6$

27) $\frac{512}{x^6}$

28) $\frac{27}{y^3}$

29) $\frac{27y^6}{x^3}$

30) $\frac{x^2}{4y^2}$

31) $9x^6y^4$

32) $25x^4y^2$

33) 512

34) 36

35) $\frac{16}{9}$

36) $\frac{81}{16}$

37) 256

38) $\frac{343}{8}$

39) $\frac{18}{x^2y^6}$

40) $\frac{35}{x^3y^5}$

41) $-\frac{12}{y^4}$

42) $-\frac{25}{x^6}$

43) $\frac{15b^6}{a^3}$

44) $\frac{20a^6}{b^5c^3}$

45) $\frac{46x^6}{y^3z^7}$

46) $\frac{16y^4}{x^3}$

47) $-\frac{3bc^3}{2a^3}$

48) 5.21×10^{-3}

49) 6.7×10^{-5}

50) 2.5×10^4

51) 3.6×10^7

52) 6

53) 5

54) 14

55) 21

56) 6

57) $5\sqrt{5}$

CHAPTER 10:

POLYNOMIALS

Math Topics that you'll learn in this chapter:

▶ Simplifying Polynomials

▶ Adding and Subtracting Polynomials

▶ Multiplying Monomials

▶ Multiplying and Dividing Monomials

▶ Multiplying a Polynomial and a Monomial

▶ Multiplying Binomials

▶ Factoring Trinomials

SIMPLIFYING POLYNOMIALS

☑ To simplify Polynomials, find "like" terms. (they have same variables with same power).

☑ Use "FOIL". (First–Out–In–Last) for binomials:

$$(x + a)(x + b) = x^2 + (b + a)x + ab$$

☑ Add or Subtract "like" terms using order of operation.

Examples:

Example 1. Simplify this expression. $x(2x + 5) + 6x =$

Solution: Use Distributive Property: $x(2x + 5) = 2x^2 + 5x$
Now, combine like terms: $x(2x + 5) + 6x = 2x^2 + 5x + 6x = 2x^2 + 11x$

Example 2. Simplify this expression. $(x + 2)(x + 3) =$

Solution: First, apply the FOIL method: $(a + b)(c + d) = ac + ad + bc + bd$
$(x + 2)(x + 3) = x^2 + 3x + 2x + 6$
Now combine like terms: $x^2 + 3x + 2x + 6 = x^2 + 5x + 6$

Example 3. Simplify this expression. $4x(2x - 3) + 6x^2 - 4x =$

Solution: Use Distributive Property: $4x(2x - 3) = 8x^2 - 12x$
Then: $4x(2x - 3) + 6x^2 - 4x = 8x^2 - 12x + 6x^2 - 4x$
Now combine like terms: $8x^2 + 6x^2 = 14x^2$, and $-12x - 4x = -16x$
The simplified form of the expression: $8x^2 - 12x + 6x^2 - 4x = 14x^2 - 16x$

ADDING AND SUBTRACTING POLYNOMIALS

☑ Adding polynomials is just a matter of combining like terms, with some order of operations considerations thrown in.

☑ Be careful with the minus signs, and don't confuse addition and multiplication!

☑ For subtracting polynomials, sometimes you need to use the Distributive Property: $a(b + c) = ab + ac$, $a(b - c) = ab - ac$

Examples:

Example 1. Simplify the expressions. $(x^3 - 3x^4) - (2x^4 - 5x^3) =$

Solution: First, use Distributive Property:

$-(2x^4 - 5x^3) = -1(2x^4 - 5x^3) = -2x^4 + 5x^3$

$\rightarrow (x^3 - 3x^4) - (2x^4 - 5x^3) = x^3 - 3x^4 - 2x^4 + 5x^3$

Now combine like terms: $x^3 + 5x^3 = 6x^3$ and $-3x^4 - 2x^4 = -5x^4$

Then: $(x^3 - 3x^4) - (2x^4 - 5x^3) = x^3 - 3x^4 - 2x^4 + 5x^3 = 6x^3 - 5x^4$

Write the answer in standard form: $6x^3 - 5x^4 = -5x^4 + 6x^3$

Example 2. Add expressions. $(2x^3 - 4) + (6x^3 - 2x^2) =$

Solution: Remove parentheses:

$(2x^3 - 4) + (6x^3 - 2x^2) = 2x^3 - 4 + 6x^3 - 2x^2$

Now combine like terms: $2x^3 - 4 + 6x^3 - 2x^2 = 8x^3 - 2x^2 - 4$

Example 3. Simplify the expressions. $(8x^2 - 3x^3) - (2x^2 + 5x^3) =$

Solution: First, use Distributive Property:

$-(2x^2 + 5x^3) = -2x^2 - 5x^3 \rightarrow (8x^2 - 3x^3) - (2x^2 + 5x^3) = 8x^2 - 3x^3 - 2x^2 - 5x^3$

Now combine like terms and write in standard form:

$8x^2 - 3x^3 - 2x^2 - 5x^3 = -8x^3 + 6x^2$

MULTIPLYING MONOMIALS

- ✓ A monomial is a polynomial with just one term: Examples: $2x$ or $7y^2$.

- ✓ When you multiply monomials, first multiply the coefficients (a number placed before and multiplying the variable) and then multiply the variables using multiplication property of exponents.

$$x^a \times x^b = x^{a+b}$$

Examples:

Example 1. Multiply expressions. $5xy^4z^2 \times 3x^2y^5z^3$

Solution: Find the same variables and use multiplication property of exponents: $x^a \times x^b = x^{a+b}$
$x \times x^2 = x^{1+2} = x^3$, $y^4 \times y^5 = y^{4+5} = y^9$ and $z^2 \times z^3 = z^{2+3} = z^5$
Then, multiply coefficients and variables: $5xy^4z^2 \times 3x^2y^5z^3 = 15x^3y^9z^5$

Example 2. Multiply expressions. $-2a^5b^4 \times 8a^3b^4 =$

Solution: Use the multiplication property of exponents: $x^a \times x^b = x^{a+b}$
$a^5 \times a^3 = a^{5+3} = a^8$ and $b^4 \times b^4 = b^{4+4} = b^8$
Then: $-2a^5b^4 \times 8a^3b^4 = -16a^8b^8$

Example 3. Multiply. $7xy^3z^5 \times 4x^2y^4z^3$

Solution: Use the multiplication property of exponents: $x^a \times x^b = x^{a+b}$
$x \times x^2 = x^{1+2} = x^3$, $y^3 \times y^4 = y^{3+4} = y^7$ and $z^5 \times z^3 = z^{5+3} = z^8$
Then: $7xy^3z^5 \times 4x^2y^5z^3 = 28x^3y^7z^8$

Example 4. Simplify. $(5a^6b^3)(-9a^7b^2) =$

Solution: Use the multiplication property of exponents: $x^a \times x^b = x^{a+b}$
$a^6 \times a^7 = a^{6+7} = a^{13}$ and $b^3 \times b^2 = b^{3+2} = b^5$
Then: $(5a^6b^3) \times (-9a^6b^2) = -45a^{13}b^5$

MULTIPLYING AND DIVIDING MONOMIALS

✓ When you divide or multiply two monomials, you need to divide or multiply their coefficients and then divide or multiply their variables.

✓ In case of exponents with the same base, for Division, subtract their powers, for Multiplication, add their powers.

✓ Exponent's Multiplication and Division rules:

$$x^a \times x^b = x^{a+b}, \qquad \frac{x^a}{x^b} = x^{a-b}$$

Examples:

Example 1. Multiply expressions. $(-5x^8)(4x^6) =$

Solution: Use multiplication property of exponents:
$x^a \times x^b = x^{a+b} \rightarrow x^8 \times x^6 = x^{14}$
Then: $(-5x^5)(4x^4) = -20x^{14}$

Example 2. Divide expressions. $\frac{14x^5y^4}{2xy^3} =$

Solution: Use division property of exponents:
$\frac{x^a}{x^b} = x^{a-b} \rightarrow \frac{x^5}{x} = x^{5-1} = x^4$ and $\frac{y^4}{y^3} = y$
Then: $\frac{14x^5y^4}{2xy^3} = 7x^4y$

Example 3. Divide expressions. $\frac{56a^8b^3}{8ab^3}$

Solution: Use division property of exponents:
$\frac{x^a}{x^b} = x^{a-b} \rightarrow \frac{a^8}{a} = a^{8-1} = a^7$ and $\frac{b^3}{b^3} = 1$
Then: $\frac{56a^8b^3}{8ab^3} = 7a^7$

MULTIPLYING A POLYNOMIAL AND A MONOMIAL

☑ When multiplying monomials, use the product rule for exponents.

$$x^a \times x^b = x^{a+b}$$

☑ When multiplying a monomial by a polynomial, use the distributive property.

$$a \times (b + c) = a \times b + a \times c = ab + ac$$
$$a \times (b - c) = a \times b - a \times c = ab - ac$$

Examples:

Example 1. Multiply expressions. $5x(3x - 2)$

Solution: Use Distributive Property:
$5x(3x - 2) = 5x \times 3x - 5x \times (-2) = 15x^2 - 10x$

Example 2. Multiply expressions. $x(2x^2 + 3y^2)$

Solution: Use Distributive Property:
$x(2x^2 + 3y^2) = x \times 2x^2 + x \times 3y^2 = 2x^3 + 3xy^2$

Example 3. Multiply. $-4x(-5x^2 + 3x - 6)$

Solution: Use Distributive Property:
$-4x(-5x^2 + 3x - 6) = (-4x)(-5x^2) + (-4x) \times (3x) + (-4x) \times (-6) =$
Now simplify:
$(-4x)(-5x^2) + (-4x) \times (3x) + (-4x) \times (-6) = 20x^3 - 12x^2 + 24x$

MULTIPLYING BINOMIALS

☑ A binomial is a polynomial that is the sum or the difference of two terms, each of which is a monomial.

☑ To multiply two binomials, use the "FOIL" method. (First–Out–In–Last)

$$(x + a)(x + b) = x \times x + x \times b + a \times x + a \times b = x^2 + bx + ax + ab$$

Examples:

Example 1. Multiply Binomials. $(x + 2)(x - 4) =$

Solution: Use "FOIL". (First–Out–In–Last):
$(x + 2)(x - 4) = x^2 - 4x + 2x - 8$
Then combine like terms: $x^2 - 4x + 2x - 8 = x^2 - 2x - 8$

Example 2. Multiply. $(x - 5)(x - 2) =$

Solution: Use "FOIL". (First–Out–In–Last):
$(x - 5)(x - 2) = x^2 - 2x - 5x + 10$
Then simplify: $x^2 - 2x - 5x + 10 = x^2 - 7x + 10$

Example 3. Multiply. $(x - 3)(x + 6) =$

Solution: Use "FOIL". (First–Out–In–Last):
$(x - 3)(x + 6) = x^2 + 6x - 3x - 18$
Then simplify: $x^2 + 6x - 3x - 18 = x^2 + 3x - 18$

Example 4. Multiply Binomials. $(x + 8)(x + 4) =$

Solution: Use "FOIL". (First–Out–In–Last):
$(x + 8)(x + 4) = x^2 + 4x + 8x + 32$
Then combine like terms: $x^2 + 4x + 8x + 32 = x^2 + 12x + 32$

FACTORING TRINOMIALS

To factor trinomials, you can use following methods:

☑ "FOIL": $(x + a)(x + b) = x^2 + (b + a)x + ab$

☑ "Difference of Squares":

$$a^2 - b^2 = (a + b)(a - b)$$
$$a^2 + 2ab + b^2 = (a + b)(a + b)$$
$$a^2 - 2ab + b^2 = (a - b)(a - b)$$

☑ "Reverse FOIL": $x^2 + (b + a)x + ab = (x + a)(x + b)$

Examples:

Example 1. Factor this trinomial. $x^2 - 2x - 8$

Solution: Break the expression into groups. You need to find two numbers that their product is -8 and their sum is -2. (remember "Reverse FOIL": $x^2 + (b + a)x + ab = (x + a)(x + b)$). Those two numbers are 2 and -4. Then: $x^2 - 2x - 8 = (x^2 + 2x) + (-4x - 8)$
Now factor out x from $x^2 + 2x : x(x + 2)$, and factor out -4 from $-4x - 8: -4(x + 2)$; Then: $(x^2 + 2x) + (-4x - 8) = x(x + 2) - 4(x + 2)$
Now factor out like term: $(x + 2)$. Then: $(x + 2)(x - 4)$

Example 2. Factor this trinomial. $x^2 - 2x - 24$

Solution: Break the expression into groups: $(x^2 + 4x) + (-6x - 24)$
Now factor out x from $x^2 + 4x : x(x + 4)$, and factor out -6 from $-6x - 24: -6(x + 4)$; Then: $(x + 4) - 6(x + 4)$, now factor out like term: $(x = 4) \rightarrow x(x + 4) - 6(x + 4) = (x + 4)(x - 6)$

CHAPTER 10: PRACTICES

✎ Simplify each polynomial.

1) $2(5x + 7) =$

2) $6(3x - 9) =$

3) $x(6x + 3) + 4x =$

4) $2x(x + 8) + 6x =$

5) $8x(2x + 1) - 6x =$

6) $5x(4x - 2) + 2x^2 - 1 =$

7) $4x^2 - 6 - 8x(2x + 7) =$

8) $7x^2 + 9 - 3x(x + 4) =$

✎ Add or subtract polynomials.

9) $(5x^2 + 4) + (3x^2 - 6) =$

10) $(2x^2 - 7x) - (4x^2 + 3x) =$

11) $(8x^3 - 5x^2) + (2x^3 - 6x^2) =$

12) $(3x^3 - 6x) - (7x^3 - 2x) =$

13) $(15x^3 + 3x^2) + (12x^2 - 9) =$

14) $(5x^3 - 8) - (2x^3 - 9x^2) =$

15) $(6x^3 + 2x) + (3x^3 - 2x) =$

16) $(3x^3 - 7x) - (4x^3 + 6x) =$

✎ Find the products. (Multiplying Monomials)

17) $6x^2 \times 4x^3 =$

18) $5x^4 \times 6x^3 =$

19) $-5a^4b \times 4ab^3 =$

20) $(-6x^3yz) \times (-5xy^2z^4) =$

21) $-a^5bc \times a^2b^4 =$

22) $7u^3t^2 \times (-8ut) =$

23) $10x^2z \times 4xy^3 =$

24) $12x^3z \times 2xy^5 =$

25) $-4a^3bc \times a^4b^3 =$

26) $8x^6y^2 \times (-10xy) =$

✍ Simplify each expression. (Multiplying and Dividing Monomials)

27) $(6x^2y^3)(9x^4y^2) =$

28) $(3x^3y^2)(7x^4y^3) =$

29) $(12x^8y^5)(4x^5y^7) =$

30) $(10a^3b^2)(5a^3b^8) =$

31) $\dfrac{32x^4y^2}{8x^3y} =$

32) $\dfrac{48x^5y^6}{6x^2y} =$

33) $\dfrac{72x^{15}y^{10}}{9x^8y^6} =$

34) $\dfrac{200x^8y^{12}}{5x^4y^8} =$

✍ Find each product. (Multiplying a Polynomial and a Monomial)

35) $2x(4x - y) =$

36) $6x(2x + 5y) =$

37) $6x(x - 9y) =$

38) $x(4x^2 + 3x - 8) =$

39) $6x(-2x^2 + 6x + 3) =$

40) $9x(3x^2 - 6x - 10) =$

✍ Find each product. (Multiplying Binomials)

41) $(x - 4)(x + 4) =$

42) $(x - 6)(x - 5) =$

43) $(x + 8)(x + 2) =$

44) $(x - 8)(x + 9) =$

45) $(x + 4)(x - 6) =$

46) $(x - 12)(x + 4) =$

✍ Factor each trinomial.

47) $x^2 + x - 12 =$

48) $x^2 + 3x - 10 =$

49) $x^2 - 10x - 24 =$

50) $x^2 + 19x + 48 =$

51) $2x^2 - 14x + 24 =$

52) $3x^2 + 3x - 18 =$

CHAPTER 10: ANSWERS

1) $10x + 14$

2) $18x - 54$

3) $6x^2 + 7x$

4) $2x^2 + 22x$

5) $16x^2 + 2x$

6) $22x^2 - 10x - 1$

7) $-12x^2 - 56x - 6$

8) $4x^2 - 12x + 9$

9) $8x^2 - 2$

10) $-2x^2 - 10x$

11) $10x^3 - 11x^2$

12) $-4x^3 - 4x$

13) $15x^3 + 15x^2 - 9$

14) $3x^3 + 9x^2 - 8$

15) $9x^3$

16) $-x^3 - 13x$

17) $24x^5$

18) $30x^7$

19) $-20a^5b^4$

20) $30x^4y^3z^5$

21) $-a^7b^5c$

22) $-56u^4t^3$

23) $40x^3y^3z$

24) $24x^4y^5z$

25) $-4a^7b^4c$

26) $-80x^7y^3$

27) $54x^6y^5$

28) $21x^7y^5$

29) $48x^{13}y^{12}$

30) $50a^6b^{10}$

31) $4xy$

32) $8x^3y^5$

33) $8x^7y^4$

34) $40x^4y^4$

35) $8x^2 - 2xy$

36) $12x^2 + 30xy$

37) $6x^2 - 54xy$

38) $4x^3 + 3x^2 - 8x$

39) $-12x^3 + 36x^2 + 18x$

40) $27x^3 - 54x^2 - 90x$

41) $x^2 - 16$

42) $x^2 - 11x + 30$

43) $x^2 + 10x + 16$

44) $x^2 + x - 72$

45) $x^2 - 2x - 24$

46) $x^2 - 8x - 48$

47) $(x + 4)(x - 3)$

48) $(x + 5)(x - 2)$

49) $(x - 12)(x + 2)$

50) $(x + 16)(x + 3)$

51) $(2x - 8)(x - 3)$

52) $(3x - 6)(x + 3)$

CHAPTER 11:

GEOMETRY AND SOLID FIGURES

Math Topics that you'll learn in this chapter:

▶ The Pythagorean Theorem

▶ Triangles

▶ Polygons

▶ Circles

▶ Trapezoids

▶ Cubes

▶ Rectangle Prisms

▶ Cylinder

THE PYTHAGOREAN THEOREM

☑ You can use the Pythagorean Theorem to find a missing side in a right triangle.

☑ In any right triangle: $a^2 + b^2 = c^2$

Examples:

Example 1. Right triangle ABC (not shown) has two legs of lengths 6 cm (AB) and 8 cm (AC). What is the length of the hypotenuse of the triangle (side BC)?

Solution: Use Pythagorean Theorem: $a^2 + b^2 = c^2$, $a = 6$, and $b = 8$

Then: $a^2 + b^2 = c^2 \rightarrow 6^2 + 8^2 = c^2 \rightarrow 36 + 64 = c^2 \rightarrow 100 = c^2 \rightarrow c = \sqrt{100} = 10$

The length of the hypotenuse is 10 cm.

Example 2. Find the hypotenuse of this triangle.

Solution: Use Pythagorean Theorem: $a^2 + b^2 = c^2$

Then: $a^2 + b^2 = c^2 \rightarrow 12^2 + 5^2 = c^2 \rightarrow 144 + 25 = c^2$

$c^2 = 169 \rightarrow c = \sqrt{169} = 13$

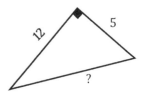

Example 3. Find the length of the missing side in this triangle.

Solution: Use Pythagorean Theorem: $a^2 + b^2 = c^2$

Then: $a^2 + b^2 = c^2 \rightarrow 3^2 + b^2 = 5^2 \rightarrow 9 + b^2 = 25 \rightarrow$

$b^2 = 25 - 9 \rightarrow b^2 = 16 \rightarrow b = \sqrt{16} = 4$

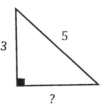

TRIANGLES

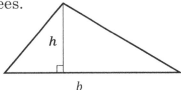

☑ In any triangle, the sum of all angles is 180 degrees.

☑ Area of a triangle $= \frac{1}{2}(base \times height)$

Examples:

What is the area of the following triangles?

Example 1.

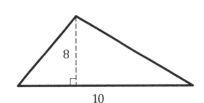

Solution: Use the area formula:
Area $= \frac{1}{2}(base \times height)$

$base = 10$ and $height = 8$

Area $= \frac{1}{2}(10 \times 8) = \frac{1}{2}(80) = 40$

Example 2.

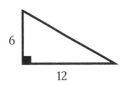

Solution: Use the area formula:
Area $= \frac{1}{2}(base \times height)$

$base = 12$ and $height = 6$; Area $= \frac{1}{2}(12 \times 6) = \frac{72}{2} = 36$

Example 3. What is the missing angle in this triangle?

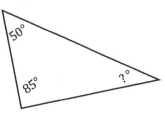

Solution:

In any triangle, the sum of all angles is 180 degrees. Let x be the missing angle.

Then: $50 + 85 + x = 180$;

$\rightarrow 135 + x = 180 \rightarrow x = 180 - 135 = 45$

The missing angle is 45 degrees.

POLYGONS

☑ The perimeter of a square = $4 \times side = 4s$

☑ The perimeter of a rectangle= $2(width + length)$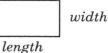

☑ The perimeter of a trapezoid= $a + b + c + d$

☑ The perimeter of a regular hexagon = $6a$

☑ The perimeter of a parallelogram = $2(l + w)$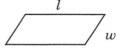

Examples:

Example 1. Find the perimeter of following regular hexagon.

Solution: Since the hexagon is regular, all sides are equal.
Then: The perimeter of a hexagon = $6 \times (one\ side)$
The perimeter of a hexagon = $6 \times (one\ side) = 6 \times 4 = 24\ m$

Example 2. Find the perimeter of following trapezoid.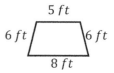

Solution: The perimeter of a trapezoid = $a + b + c + d$
The perimeter of a trapezoid = $5 + 6 + 6 + 8 = 25\ ft$

CIRCLES

☑ In a circle, variable r is usually used for the radius and d for diameter.

☑ *Area of a circle* $= \pi r^2$ *(π is about 3.14)*

☑ *Circumference of a circle* $= 2\pi r$

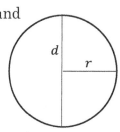

Examples:

Example 1. Find the area of this circle.

Solution:
Use area formula: *Area* $= \pi r^2$
$r = 8\ in \rightarrow Area = \pi(8)^2 = 64\pi$, $\pi = 3.14$
Then: *Area* $= 64 \times 3.14 = 200.96\ in^2$

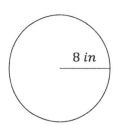

Example 2. Find the Circumference of this circle.

Solution:
Use Circumference formula: *Circumference* $= 2\pi r$
$r = 5\ cm \rightarrow Circumference = 2\pi(5) = 10\pi$
$\pi = 3.14$ Then: *Circumference* $= 10 \times 3.14 = 31.4\ cm$

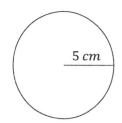

Example 3. Find the area of the circle.

Solution:
Use area formula: *Area* $= \pi r^2$,
$r = 5\ in$ then: *Area* $= \pi(5)^2 = 25\pi$, $\pi = 3.14$
Then: *Area* $= 25 \times 3.14 = 78.5$

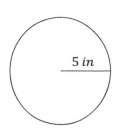

TRAPEZOIDS

☑ A quadrilateral with at least one pair of parallel sides is a trapezoid.

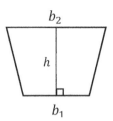

☑ Area of a trapezoid $= \frac{1}{2}h(b_1 + b_2)$

Examples:

Example 1. Calculate the area of this trapezoid.

Solution:

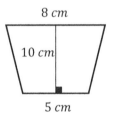

Use area formula: $A = \frac{1}{2}h(b_1 + b_2)$

$b_1 = 5\ cm$, $b_2 = 8\ cm$ and $h = 10\ cm$

Then: $A = \frac{1}{2}(10)(8 + 5) = 5(13) = 65\ cm^2$

Example 2. Calculate the area of this trapezoid.

Solution:

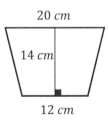

Use area formula: $A = \frac{1}{2}h(b_1 + b_2)$

$b_1 = 12\ cm$, $b_2 = 20\ cm$ and $h = 14\ cm$

Then: $A = \frac{1}{2}(14)(12 + 20) = 7(32) = 224\ cm^2$

CUBES

☑ A cube is a three-dimensional solid object bounded by six square sides.

☑ Volume is the measure of the amount of space inside of a solid figure, like a cube, ball, cylinder or pyramid.

☑ The volume of a cube = $(one\ side)^3$

☑ The surface area of a cube = $6 \times (one\ side)^2$

Examples:

Example 1. Find the volume and surface area of this cube.

Solution: Use volume formula: $volume = (one\ side)^3$
Then: $volume = (one\ side)^3 = (2)^3 = 8\ cm^3$
Use surface area formula:
$surface\ area\ of\ cube: 6(one\ side)^2 = 6(2)^2 = 6(4) = 24\ cm^2$

2 cm

Example 2. Find the volume and surface area of this cube.

Solution: Use volume formula: $volume = (one\ side)^3$
Then: $volume = (one\ side)^3 = (5)^3 = 125\ cm^3$
Use surface area formula:
$surface\ area\ of\ cube: 6(one\ side)^2 = 6(5)^2 = 6(25) = 150\ cm^2$

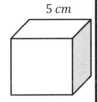
5 cm

Example 3. Find the volume and surface area of this cube.

Solution: Use volume formula: $volume = (one\ side)^3$
Then: $volume = (one\ side)^3 = (7)^3 = 343\ m^3$
Use surface area formula:
$surface\ area\ of\ cube: 6(one\ side)^2 = 6(7)^2 = 6(49) = 294\ m^2$

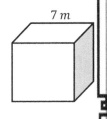
7 m

RECTANGULAR PRISMS

☑ A rectangular prism is a solid 3-dimensional object with six rectangular faces.

☑ The volume of a Rectangular prism = $Length \times Width \times Height$

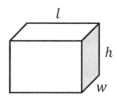

$Volume = l \times w \times h$

$Surface\ area = 2 \times (wh + lw + lh)$

Examples:

Example 1. Find the volume and surface area of this rectangular prism.

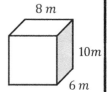

Solution: Use volume formula: $Volume = l \times w \times h$

Then: $Volume = 8 \times 6 \times 10 = 480\ m^3$

Use surface area formula: $Surface\ area = 2 \times (wh + lw + lh)$

Then: $Surface\ area = 2 \times ((6 \times 10) + (8 \times 6) + (8 \times 10))$

$= 2 \times (60 + 48 + 80) = 2 \times (188) = 376\ m^2$

Example 2. Find the volume and surface area of this rectangular prism.

Solution: Use volume formula: $Volume = l \times w \times h$

Then: $Volume = 10 \times 8 \times 12 = 960\ m^3$

Use surface area formula: $Surface\ area = 2 \times (wh + lw + lh)$

Then: $Surface\ area = 2 \times ((8 \times 12) + (10 \times 8) + (10 \times 12))$

$= 2 \times (96 + 80 + 120) = 2 \times (296) = 592\ m^2$

CYLINDER

☑ A cylinder is a solid geometric figure with straight parallel sides and a circular or oval cross-section.

☑ *Volume of a Cylinder* $= \pi(radius)^2 \times height$, $\pi \approx 3.14$

☑ *Surface area of a cylinder* $= 2\pi r^2 + 2\pi rh$

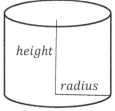

Examples:

Example 1. Find the volume and Surface area of the follow Cylinder.

Solution: Use volume formula:

$Volume = \pi(radius)^2 \times height$

Then: $Volume = \pi(3)^2 \times 8 = 9\pi \times 8 = 72\pi$

$\pi = 3.14$ then: $Volume = 72\pi = 72 \times 3.14 = 226.08 \ cm^3$

Use surface area formula: $Surface \ area = 2\pi r^2 + 2\pi rh$

Then: $2\pi(3)^2 + 2\pi(3)(8) = 2\pi(9) + 2\pi(24) = 18\pi + 48\pi = 66\pi$

$\pi = 3.14$ Then: $Surface \ area = 66 \times 3.14 = 207.24 \ cm^2$

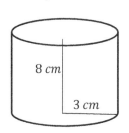

Example 2. Find the volume and Surface area of the follow Cylinder.

Solution: Use volume formula:

$Volume = \pi(radius)^2 \times height$

Then: $Volume = \pi(2)^2 \times 6 = \pi 4 \times 6 = 24\pi$

$\pi = 3.14$ then: $Volume = 24\pi = 75.36 \ cm^3$

Use surface area formula: $Surface \ area = 2\pi r^2 + 2\pi rh$

Then: $= 2\pi(2)^2 + 2\pi(2)(6) = 2\pi(4) + 2\pi(12) = 8\pi + 24\pi = 32\pi$

$\pi = 3.14$ then: $Surface \ area = 32 \times 3.14 = 100.48 \ cm^2$

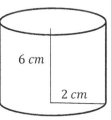

CHAPTER 11: PRACTICES

✍ Find the missing side?

1)

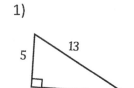

13
5
?

2)

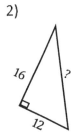

16
?
12

3)

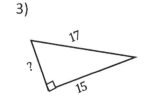

17
?
15

4)

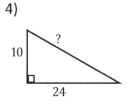

?
10
24

✍ Find the measure of the unknown angle in each triangle.

5)

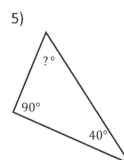

?°
90°
40°

6)

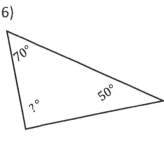

70°
?°
50°

7)

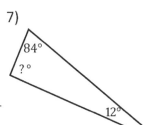

84°
?°
12°

8)

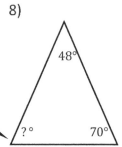

48°
?°
70°

✍ Find the area of each triangle.

9)

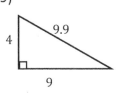

9.9
4
9

10)

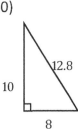

12.8
10
8

11)

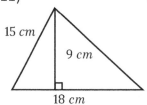

15 cm
9 cm
18 cm

12)

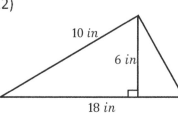

10 in
6 in
18 in

✍ Find the perimeter or circumference of each shape.

13)

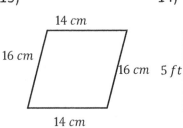

14 cm
16 cm
16 cm
14 cm

14)

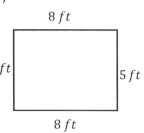

8 ft
5 ft
5 ft
8 ft

15)

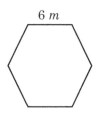

6 in

16) *regular hexagon*

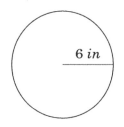

6 m

✍ **Find the area of each trapezoid.**

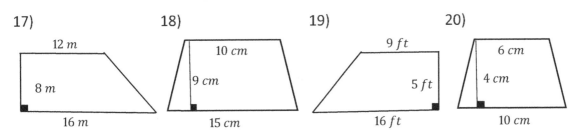

17) 12 m 8 m 16 m

18) 10 cm 9 cm 15 cm

19) 9 ft 5 ft 16 ft

20) 6 cm 4 cm 10 cm

✍ **Find the volume of each cube.**

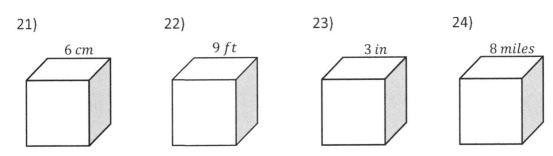

21) 6 cm

22) 9 ft

23) 3 in

24) 8 miles

✍ **Find the volume of each Rectangular Prism.**

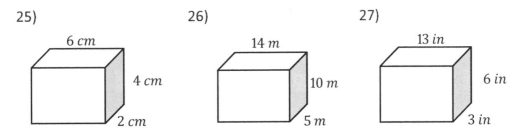

25) 6 cm 4 cm 2 cm

26) 14 m 10 m 5 m

27) 13 in 6 in 3 in

✍ **Find the volume of each Cylinder. Round your answer to the nearest tenth. ($\pi = 3.14$)**

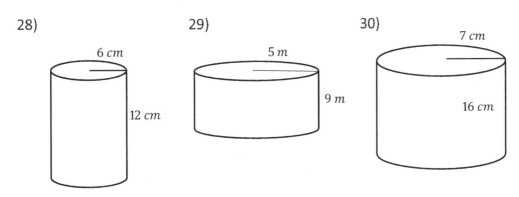

28) 6 cm 12 cm

29) 5 m 9 m

30) 7 cm 16 cm

CHAPTER 11: ANSWERS

1) 12

2) 20

3) 8

4) 26

5) 50

6) 60

7) 84

8) 62

9) 18

10) 40

11) $81\ cm^2$

12) $54 in^2$

13) $60\ cm$

14) $26\ ft$

15) $12\pi \approx 37.68\ in$

16) $36\ m$

17) $112\ m^2$

18) $112.5\ cm^2$

19) $62.5\ ft^2$

20) $32\ cm^2$

21) $216\ cm^3$

22) $729\ ft^3$

23) $27\ in^3$

24) $512\ mi^3$

25) $48\ cm^3$

26) $700\ m^3$

27) $234\ in^3$

28) $1,356.5\ cm^3$

29) $706.5\ m^3$

30) $2,461.8\ cm^3$

CHAPTER 12:

STATISTICS

Math Topics that you'll learn in this chapter:

▶ Mean, Median, Mode, and Range of the Given Data

▶ Pie Graph

▶ Probability Problems

▶ Permutations and Combinations

MEAN, MEDIAN, MODE, AND RANGE OF THE GIVEN DATA

☑ Mean: $\dfrac{sum\ of\ the\ data}{total\ number\ of\ data\ entires}$

☑ Mode: the value in the list that appears most often

☑ Median: is the middle number of a group of numbers arranged in order by size.

☑ Range: the difference of the largest value and smallest value in the list

Examples:

Example 1. What is the mode of these numbers? $4, 5, 7, 5, 7, 4, 0, 4$

Solution: Mode: the value in the list that appears most often.
Therefore, the mode is number 4. There are three number 4 in the data.

Example 2. What is the median of these numbers? $5, 10, 14, 9, 16, 19, 6$

Solution: Write the numbers in order: $5, 6, 9, 10, 14, 16, 19$
The median is the number in the middle. Therefore, the median is 10.

Example 3. What is the mean of these numbers? $8, 2, 8, 5, 3, 2, 4, 8$

Solution: Mean: $\dfrac{sum\ of\ the\ data}{total\ number\ of\ data\ entires} = \dfrac{8+2+8+5+3+2+4+8}{8} = 5$

Example 4. What is the range in this list? $4, 9, 13, 8, 15, 18, 5$

Solution: Range is the difference of the largest value and smallest value in the list. The largest value is 18 and the smallest value is 4.
Then: $18 - 4 = 14$

PIE GRAPH

☑ A Pie Chart is a circle chart divided into sectors, each sector represents the relative size of each value.

☑ Pie charts represent a snapshot of how a group is broken down into smaller pieces.

Example:

A library has 820 books that include Mathematics, Physics, Chemistry, English and History. Use the following graph to answer the questions.

Example 1. What is the number of Mathematics books?

Solution: Number of total books = 820

Percent of Mathematics books = 30% = 0.30

Then, the number of Mathematics books: $0.30 \times 820 = 246$

Example 2. What is the number of History books?

Solution: Number of total books = 820

Percent of History books = 10% = 0.10

Then: $0.10 \times 820 = 82$

Example 3. What is the number of Chemistry books?

Solution: Number of total books = 820

Percent of Chemistry books = 20% = 0.20

Then: $0.20 \times 820 = 164$

PROBABILITY PROBLEMS

- ⊘ Probability is the likelihood of something happening in the future. It is expressed as a number between zero (can never happen) to 1 (will always happen).

- ⊘ Probability can be expressed as a fraction, a decimal, or a percent.

- ⊘ Probability formula: $Probability = \frac{number\ of\ desired\ outcomes}{number\ of\ total\ outcomes}$

Examples:

Example 1. Anita's trick–or–treat bag contains 12 pieces of chocolate, 18 suckers, 18 pieces of gum, 24 pieces of licorice. If she randomly pulls a piece of candy from her bag, what is the probability of her pulling out a piece of sucker?

Solution: Probability $= \frac{number\ of\ desired\ outcomes}{number\ of\ total\ outcomes}$

Probability of pulling out a piece of sucker $= \frac{18}{12 + 18 + 18 + 24} = \frac{18}{72} = \frac{1}{4}$

Example 2. A bag contains 20 balls: four green, five black, eight blue, a brown, a red and one white. If 19 balls are removed from the bag at random, what is the probability that a brown ball has been removed?

Solution: If 19 balls are removed from the bag at random, there will be one ball in the bag. The probability of choosing a brown ball is 1 out of 20. Therefore, the probability of not choosing a brown ball is 19 out of 20 and the probability of having not a brown ball after removing 19 balls is the same. The answer is $\frac{19}{20}$.

PERMUTATIONS AND COMBINATIONS

☑ Factorials are products, indicated by an exclamation mark. For example, $4! = 4 \times 3 \times 2 \times 1$(Remember that $0!$ is defined to be equal to 1.)

☑ Permutations: The number of ways to choose a sample of k elements from a set of n distinct objects where order does matter, and replacements are not allowed. For a permutation problem, use this formula:

$$_n\mathrm{P}k = \frac{n!}{(n-k)!}$$

☑ Combination: The number of ways to choose a sample of r elements from a set of n distinct objects where order does not matter, and replacements are not allowed. For a combination problem, use this formula:

$$_n\mathrm{C}r = \frac{n!}{r!\,(n-r)!}$$

Examples:

Example 1. How many ways can the first and second place be awarded to 8 people?

Solution: Since the order matters, (the first and second place are different!) we need to use permutation formula where n is 10 and k is 2. Then: $\frac{n!}{(n-k)!} = \frac{8!}{(8-2)!} = \frac{8!}{6!} = \frac{8\times7\times6!}{6!}$, remove 6! from both sides of the fraction. Then: $\frac{8\times7\times6!}{6!} = 8 \times 7 = 56$

Example 2. How many ways can we pick a team of 2 people from a group of 6?

Solution: Since the order doesn't matter, we need to use a combination formula where n is 8 and r is 3. Then:$\frac{n!}{r!\,(n-r)!} = \frac{6!}{2!\,(6-2)!} = \frac{6!}{2!\,(4)!} = \frac{6\times5\times4!}{2!\,(4)!} = \frac{6\times5}{2\times1} = \frac{30}{2} = 15$

CHAPTER 12: PRACTICES

✍ Find the values of the Given Data.

1) $7, 10, 4, 2, 7$

    Mode: _____   Range: _____

    Mean: _____   Median: _____

2) $4, 8, 2, 9, 8, 5$

    Mode: _____   Range: _____

    Mean: _____   Median: _____

3) $12, 2, 6, 10, 6, 15$

    Mode: _____   Range: _____

    Mean: _____   Median: _____

4) $12, 5, 1, 10, 2, 11, 1$

    Mode: _____   Range: _____

    Mean: _____   Median: _____

✍ The circle graph below shows all Bob's expenses for last month. Bob spent $896 on his Rent last month.

5) How much did Bob's total expenses last month? _____

6) How much did Bob spend for foods last month? _____

7) How much did Bob spend for his bills last month?

_____

8) How much did Bob spend on his car last month? _____

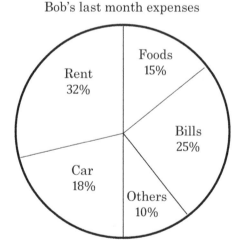

Bob's last month expenses

✎ Solve.

9) Bag A contains 6 red marbles and 9 green marbles. Bag B contains 4 black marbles and 7 orange marbles. What is the probability of selecting a green marble at random from bag A? What is the probability of selecting a black marble at random from Bag B?

_____   _____

✎ Solve.

10) Susan is baking cookies. She uses sugar, flour, butter, and eggs. How many different orders of ingredients can she try? _____

11) Jason is planning for his vacation. He wants to go to museum, go to the beach, and play volleyball. How many different ways of ordering are there for him? _____

12) In how many ways can a team of 8 basketball players choose a captain and co-captain? _____

13) How many ways can you give 6 balls to your 8 friends? _____

14) A professor is going to arrange her 6 students in a straight line. In how many ways can she do this? _____

15) In how many ways can a teacher chooses 5 out of 13 students? _____

CHAPTER 12: ANSWERS

1) Mode: 7, Range: 8, Mean: 6, Median: 7

2) Mode: 8, Range:7, Mean: 6, Median: 6.5

3) Mode: 6, Range: 13, Mean: 8.5, Median: 8

4) Mode: 1, Range: 11, Mean: 6, Median: 5

5) $2,800

6) $420

7) $700

8) $504

9) $\frac{3}{5}, \frac{4}{11}$

10) 24

11) 6

12) 56 (it's a permutation problem)

13) 28 (it's a combination problem)

14) 720

15) 1,287 (it's a combination problem)

CHAPTER 13:

FUNCTIONS OPERATIONS

Math Topics that you'll learn in this chapter:

- ☑ Function Notation
- ☑ Adding and Subtracting Functions
- ☑ Multiplying and Dividing Functions
- ☑ Composition of Functions

FUNCTION NOTATION AND EVALUATION

☑ Functions are mathematical operations that assign unique outputs to given inputs.

☑ Function notation is the way a function is written. It is meant to be a precise way of giving information about the function without a rather lengthy written explanation.

☑ The most popular function notation is $f(x)$ which is read "f of x". Any letter can name a function. for example: $g(x)$, $h(x)$, etc.

☑ To evaluate a function, plug in the input (the given value or expression) for the function's variable (place holder, x).

Examples:

Example 1. Evaluate: $h(n) = 2n - 2$, find $h(2)$

Solution: Substitute n with 2:
Then: $h(n) = 2n - 2 \rightarrow h(2) = 2(2) - 2 \rightarrow h(2) = 4 - 2 = 2$

Example 2. Evaluate: $w(x) = 5x - 1$, find $w(3)$.

Solution: Substitute x with 3:
Then: $w(x) = 5x - 1 \rightarrow w(3) = 5(3) - 1 = 15 - 1 = 14$

Example 3. Evaluate: $f(x) = x^2 - 2$, find $f(2)$.

Solution: Substitute x with 2:
Then: $f(x) = x^2 - 2 \rightarrow f(2) = (2)^2 - 2 = 4 - 2 = 2$

Example 4. Evaluate: $p(x) = 2x^2 - 4$, find $p(3a)$.

Solution: Substitute x with $3a$:
Then: $p(x) = 2x^2 - 4 \rightarrow p(3a) = 2(3a)^2 - 4 \rightarrow p(3a) = 2(9a^2) - 4 = 18a^2 - 4$

ADDING AND SUBTRACTING FUNCTIONS

✅ Just like we can add and subtract numbers and expressions, we can add or subtract two functions and simplify or evaluate them. The result is a new function.

✅ For two functions $f(x)$ and $g(x)$, we can create two new functions:

$$(f + g)(x) = f(x) + g(x) \text{ and } (f - g)(x) = f(x) - g(x)$$

Examples:

Example 1. $g(x) = a - 1$, $f(a) = a + 2$, Find: $(g + f)(a)$

Solution: $(g + f)(a) = g(a) + f(a)$
Then: $(g + f)(a) = (a - 1) + (a + 2) = 2a + 1$

Example 2. $f(x) = 2x - 2$, $g(x) = x - 4$, Find: $(f - g)(x)$

Solution: $(f - g)(x) = f(x) - g(x)$
Then: $(f - g)(x) = (2x - 2) - (x - 4) = 2x - 2 - x + 4 = x + 2$

Example 3. $g(x) = x^2 - 4$, $f(x) = 2x + 3$, Find: $(g + f)(x)$

Solution: $(g + f)(x) = g(x) + f(x)$
Then: $(g + f)(x) = (x^2 - 4) + (2x + 3) = x^2 + 2x - 1$

Example 4. $f(x) = 2x^2 + 5$, $g(x) = 3x - 1$, Find: $(f - g)(5)$

Solution: $(f - g)(x) = f(x) - g(x)$
Then: $(f - g)(x) = (2x^2 + 5) - (3x - 1) = 2x^2 + 5 - 3x + 1 = 2x^2 - 3x + 6$
Substitute x with 5: $(g - f)(5) = 2(5)^2 - 3(5) + 6 = 50 - 15 + 6 = 41$

MULTIPLYING AND DIVIDING FUNCTIONS

☑ Just like we can multiply and divide numbers and expressions, we can multiply and divide two functions and simplify or evaluate them.

☑ For two functions $f(x)$ and $g(x)$, we can create two new functions:

$$(f.g)(x) = f(x).g(x) \text{ and } \left(\frac{f}{g}\right)(x) = \frac{f(x)}{g(x)}$$

Examples:

Example 1. $g(x) = x - 2$, $f(x) = x + 3$, Find: $(g.f)(x)$

Solution: $(g.f)(x) = g(x).f(x) = (x - 2)(x + 3) = x^2 + 3x - 2x - 6$
$g(x).f(x) = x^2 + x - 6$

Example 2. $f(x) = x + 4$, $h(x) = x - 6$, Find: $\left(\frac{f}{h}\right)(x)$

Solution: $\left(\frac{f}{h}\right)(x) = \frac{f(x)}{h(x)} = \frac{x+4}{x-6}$

Example 3. $g(x) = x + 5$, $f(x) = x - 2$, Find: $(g.f)(4)$

Solution: $(g.f)(x) = g(x).f(x) = (x + 5)(x - 2) = x^2 - 2x + 5x - 10$
$g(x).f(x) = x^2 + 3x - 10$
Substitute x with 4: $(g.f)(x) = (4)^2 + 3(4) - 10 = 16 + 12 - 10 = 18$

Example 4. $f(x) = 2x + 3$, $h(x) = x + 8$, Find: $\left(\frac{f}{h}\right)(-1)$

Solution: $\left(\frac{f}{h}\right)(x) = \frac{f(x)}{h(x)} = \frac{2x+3}{x+8}$
Substitute x with -1: $\left(\frac{f}{h}\right)(x) = \frac{2x+3}{x+8} = \frac{2(-1)+3}{(-1)+8} = \frac{1}{7}$

COMPOSITION OF FUNCTIONS

☑ "Composition of functions" simply means combining two or more functions in a way where the output from one function becomes the input for the next function.

☑ The notation used for composition is: $(f o g)(x) = f\big(g(x)\big)$ and is read "f composed with g of x" or "f of g of x".

Examples:

Example 1. Using f(x) = x − 5 and g(x) = 2x, find: (fog)(x)

Solution: $(f o g)(x) = f\big(g(x)\big)$. Then: $(f o g)(x) = f\big(g(x)\big) = f(2x)$
Now find $f(2x)$ by substituting x with $2x$ in $f(x)$ function.
Then: $f(x) = x - 5$; $(x \to 2x) \to f(2x) = (2x) - 5 = 2x - 5$

Example 2. Using f(x) = x + 6 and g(x) = x − 2, find: (g o f)(−1)

Solution: $(f o g)(x) = f\big(g(x)\big)$. Then: $(g o f)(x) = g\big(f(x)\big) = g(x + 6)$, now substitute x in g(x) by (x + 6).
Then: $g(x + 6) = (x + 6) - 2 = x + 6 - 2 = x + 4$
Substitute x with −1: $(g o f)(-1) = g\big(f(x)\big) = x + 4 = -1 + 4 = 3$

Example 3. Using $f(x) = 2x - 2$ and $g(x) = 2x$, find:$f\big(g(5)\big)$

Solution: First, find g(5)): $g(x) = 2x \to g(5) = 2(5) = 10$
Then: $f\big(g(5)\big) = f(10)$. Now, find $f(10)$ by substituting x with 10 in $f(x)$ function. Then: $f\big(g(5)\big) = f(10) = 2(10) - 2 = 20 - 2 = 18$

CHAPTER 13: PRACTICES

✍ Evaluate each function.

1) $g(n) = 5n - 2$, find $g(-3)$

_____

2) $h(x) = -4x + 9$, find $h(4)$

_____

3) $k(n) = 10 - 6n$, find $k(2)$

_____

4) $g(x) = 6x - 1$, find $g(-1)$

_____

5) $k(n) = 7n - 3$, find $k(5)$

_____

6) $w(n) = -3n + 10$, find $w(6)$

_____

✍ Perform the indicated operation.

7) $f(x) = x + 3$
   $g(x) = 4x + 1$
   Find $(f - g)(x)$

_____

8) $g(x) = x - 5$
   $f(x) = -x - 6$
   Find $(g - f)(x)$

_____

9) $h(t) = 6t + 2$
   $g(t) = 3t + 4$
   Find $(h + g)(x)$

_____

10) $g(a) = 5a - 3$
    $f(a) = a^2 + 2$
    Find $(g + f)(2)$

_____

11) $g(x) = 2x - 6$
    $h(x) = 3x^2 + 1$
    Find $(g - f)(-4)$

_____

12) $h(x) = x^2 + 6$
    $g(x) = -5x + 1$
    Find $(h + g)(4)$

_____

✐ **Perform the indicated operation.**

13) $g(x) = x + 1$

    $f(x) = x + 2$

    Find $(g.f)(x)$

    _____

14) $f(x) = 3x$

    $h(x) = -x + 4$

    Find $(f.h)(x)$

    _____

15) $g(a) = a + 5$

    $h(a) = 3a - 1$

    Find $(g.h)(6)$

    _____

16) $f(x) = 2x + 3$

    $h(x) = 3x - 1$

    Find $\left(\frac{f}{h}\right)(3)$

    _____

17) $f(x) = a^2 - 1$

    $g(x) = -3 + 4a$

    Find $\left(\frac{f}{g}\right)(6)$

    _____

18) $g(a) = 3a + 6$

    $f(a) = a - 1$

    Find $\left(\frac{g}{f}\right)(4)$

    _____

✐ **Using $f(x) = 3x + 1$ and $g(x) = x - 4$, find:**

19) $g\big(f(1)\big) = $_____

20) $g\big(f(-1)\big) = $_____

21) $f\big(g(3)\big) = $_____

22) $f\big(f(6)\big) = $_____

23) $g\big(f(4)\big) = $_____

24) $g\big(f(-6)\big) = $_____

25) $g\big(f(5)\big) = $____

26) $g\big(f(-5)\big) = $____

27) $f\big(g(-2)\big) = $____

CHAPTER 13: ANSWERS

1) -17

2) -7

3) -2

4) -7

5) 32

6) -8

7) $-3x + 2$

8) $2x + 1$

9) $9t + 6$

10) 13

11) 63

12) 3

13) $x^2 + 3x + 2$

14) $-3x^2 + 12x$

15) 187

16) $\frac{9}{8}$

17) $\frac{35}{21}$

18) 6

19) 0

20) -6

21) -2

22) 58

23) 9

24) -21

25) 12

26) -18

27) -17

TIME TO TEST

Time to refine your Math skill with a practice test

In this section, there are 2 complete Arithmetic Reasoning and Mathematics Knowledge ASVAB Tests. All practice tests are paper and pencil (P&P) ASVAB tests. Take these tests to see what score you'll be able to receive on a real ASVAB test. After you've finished, score your tests using the answer keys.

Before You Start

- ❖ You'll need a pencil and a timer to take the test.
- ❖ For each question, there are four possible answers. Choose which one is best.
- ❖ It's okay to guess. There is no penalty for wrong answers.
- ❖ Use the answer sheet provided to record your answers.
- ❖ After you've finished the test, review the answer key to see where you went wrong.

Calculators are NOT permitted for the ASVAB Test

Good Luck!

ASVAB Mathematics Practice Test 1

2021

Section 1: Arithmetic Reasoning

Total number of questions: 30

Total time for this section 36 Minutes

You may NOT use a calculator on this Section.

1) Which of the following inequalities is true?

A. $\frac{3}{4} < \frac{17}{24}$

B. $\frac{2}{3} < \frac{7}{9}$

C. $\frac{3}{8} < \frac{9}{25}$

D. $\frac{11}{21} < \frac{4}{7}$

2) What is the value of 4.56×7.8?

A. 35.568

B. 36.08

C. 355.68

D. 360.80

3) 12% of what number is equal to 72?

A. 11.25

B. 112.50

C. 400

D. 600

4) Four one – foot rulers can be split among how many users to leave each with $\frac{1}{3}$ of a ruler?

A. 4

B. 6

C. 12

D. 24

5) A taxi driver earns $8 per 1-hour work. If he works 10 hours a day and in 1 hour he uses 2-liters petrol with price $1 for 1-liter. How much money does he earn in one day?

A. $90

B. $88

C. $60

D. $50

6) The following graph shows the mark of six students in mathematics. What is the mean (average) of the marks?

A. 15

B. 14

C. 13.5

D. 12.5

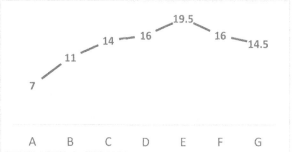

7) The price of a sofa is decreased by 20% to $476. What was its original price?

A. $480

B. $520

C. $595

D. $600

8) If 45% of a class are girls, and 25% of girls play tennis, what percent of the class play tennis?

A. 11%

B. 15%

C. 20%

D. 40%

9) If 60% of A is 30% of B, then B is what percent of A?

A. 2%

B. 20%

C. 100%

D. 200%

10) In the following graph, which of the data point is farthest from the line of best fit (not shown)?

A. $(6, 1)$

B. $(5, 4)$

C. $(3, 3)$

D. $(2, 2)$

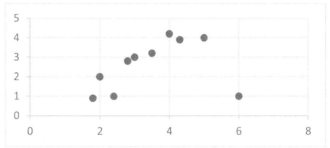

11) The ratio of boys and girls in a class is $4:7$. If there are 55 students in the class, how many more boys should be enrolled to make the ratio $1:1$?

A. 8

B. 10

C. 15

D. 20

12) Which of the following expressions has the same value as $\frac{5}{4} \times \frac{6}{2}$?

A. $\frac{6 \times 3}{4}$

B. $\frac{6 \times 2}{4}$

C. $\frac{5 \times 6}{4}$

D. $\frac{5 \times 3}{4}$

13) 35 is What percent of 20?

A. 20%

B. 25%

C. 175%

D. 190%

14) Jason needs an 70% average in his writing class to pass. On his first 4 exams, he earned scores of 68%, 72%, 85%, and 90%. What is the minimum score Jason can earn on his fifth and final test to pass?

A. 80%

B. 70%

C. 68%

D. 35%

15) How long does a 416–miles trip take moving at 65 miles per hour (*mph*)?

A. 4 *hours*

B. 4 *hours and* 24 *minutes*

C. 6 *hours and* 24 *minutes*

D. 8 *hours and* 30 *minutes*

16) The average of 6 numbers is 14. The average of 4 of those numbers is 10. What is the average of the other two numbers?

A. 10

B. 12

C. 14

D. 22

17) If 150% of a number is 75, then what is the 80% of that number?

A. 40

B. 50

C. 70

D. 85

18) $\frac{(8+6)^2}{2} + 6 = ?$

A. 110

B. 104

C. 90

D. 14

19) A rope weighs 600 grams per meter of length. What is the weight in kilograms of 14.2 meters of this rope? (1 *kilograms* = 1,000 *grams*)

A. 0.0852

B. 0.852

C. 8.52

D. 85.20

20) When 78 is divided by 5, the remainder is the same as when 45 is divided by

A. 2

B. 4

C. 5

D. 7

21) If a tree casts a 26–foot shadow at the same time that a 3 feet yardstick casts a 2–foot shadow, what is the height of the tree?

A. 24 *ft*

B. 28 *ft*

C. 39 *ft*

D. 48 *ft*

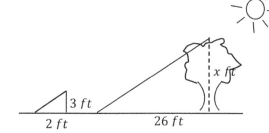

22) Jason is 9 miles ahead of Joe running at 6.5 miles per hour and Joe is running at the speed of 8 miles per hour. How long does it take Joe to catch Jason?

A. 3 *hours*

B. 4 *hours*

C. 6 *hours*

D. 8 *hours*

23) John works for an electric company. He receives a monthly salary of $4,500 plus 5% of all his monthly sales as bonus. If x is the number of all John's sales per month, which of the following represents John's monthly revenue in dollars?

A. $0.05x - 4,500$

B. $0.95x - 4,500$

C. $0.05x + 4,500$

D. $0.95x + 4,500$

24) If $x = 9$, what is the value of y in the following equation?

$$2y = \frac{2x^2}{3} + 6$$

A. 30

B. 45

C. 60

D. 120

25) John traveled 150 km in 6 hours and Alice traveled 180 km in 4 hours. What is the ratio of the average speed of John to average speed of Alice?

A. $3 : 2$

B. $2 : 3$

C. $5 : 9$

D. $5 : 6$

26) In five successive hours, a car traveled 40 km, 45 km, 50 km, 35 km and 55 km. In the next five hours, it traveled with an average speed of 50 km per hour. Find the total distance the car traveled in 10 hours.

A. 425 km

B. 450 km

C. 475 km

D. 500 km

27) The ratio of boys to girls in a school is 2:3. If there are 600 students in a school, how many boys are in the school?

A. 540

B. 360

C. 300

D. 240

28) 25 is What percent of 20?

A. 20%

B. 25%

C. 125%

D. 150%

29) Two third of 18 is equal to $\frac{2}{5}$ of what number?

A. 12

B. 20

C. 30

D. 60

30) From last year, the price of gasoline has increased from $1.25 per gallon to $1.75 per gallon. The new price is what percent of the original price?

A. 72%

B. 120%

C. 140%

D. 160%

STOP: This is the End of Section 1 of test 1.

ASVAB Mathematics Practice Test 1

2021

Section 2: Mathematics Knowledge

Total number of questions: 25

Total time for this section 24 Minutes

You may NOT use a calculator on this Section.

1) When a number is subtracted from 24 and the difference is divided by that number, the result is 3. What is the value of the number?

A. 2

B. 4

C. 6

D. 12

2) An angle is equal to one fifth of its supplement. What is the measure of that angle?

A. 20

B. 30

C. 45

D. 60

3) If the interior angles of a quadrilateral are in the ratio $1:2:3:4$, what is the measure of the smallest angle?

A. 36°

B. 72°

C. 108°

D. 144°

4) Right triangle ABC has two legs of lengths $6\ cm$ (AB) and $8\ cm$ (AC). What is the length of the third side (BC)?

A. $4\ cm$

B. $6\ cm$

C. $8\ cm$

D. $10\ cm$

5) The perimeter of the trapezoid below is 54. What is its area?

A. $252\ cm^2$

B. $234\ cm^2$

C. $216\ cm^2$

D. $130\ cm^2$

18 cm

12 cm

14 cm

6) The area of a circle is 25π. What is the circumference of the circle?

A. 5π

B. 10π

C. 32π

D. 64π

7) A boat sails 40 miles south and then 30 miles west. How far is the boat from its start point?

A. 45 $miles$

B. 50 $miles$

C. 60 $miles$

D. 70 $miles$

8) The radius of a cylinder is 8 inches and its height is 12 inches. What is the surface area of the cylinder?

A. $64\pi\ in^2$

B. $128\pi\ in^2$

C. $192\pi\ in^2$

D. $320\pi\ in^2$

9) A bank is offering 4.5% simple interest on a savings account. If you deposit $8,000, how much interest will you earn in five years?

A. $360

B. $720

C. $1,800

D. $3,600

10) Multiply and write the product in scientific notation:
$$(4.2 \times 10^6) \times (2.6 \times 10^{-5})$$

A. $1,092 \times 10$

B. 10.92×10^6

C. 109.2×10^{-5}

D. 1.092×10^2

11) If the height of a right pyramid is $12\ cm$ and its base is a square with side $6\ cm$. What is its volume?

A. $32\ cm^3$

B. $36\ cm^3$

C. $48\ cm^3$

D. $144\ cm^3$

12) What is the value of $|-13-6|-|-9+3|$?

A. 13

B. -13

C. 23

D. -23

13) Which of the following expressions is equivalent to $2x(4+2y)$?

A. $2xy+8x$

B. $8xy+8x$

C. $xy+8$

D. $4xy+8x$

14) If $y=4ab+3b^3$, what is y when $a=2$ and $b=3$?

A. 24

B. 31

C. 36

D. 105

15) Which of the following graphs represents the compound inequality $-2 < 2x - 4 < 8$?

A.
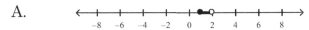

B.

C.

D.

16) A number is chosen at random from 1 to 25. Find the probability of not selecting a composite number.

A. $\frac{9}{25}$

B. $\frac{6}{5}$

C. $\frac{2}{5}$

D. 1

17) Which of the following points lies on the line $2x + 4y = 10$

A. $(2, 1)$

B. $(-1, 3)$

C. $(-2, 2)$

D. $(2, 2)$

18) A ladder leans against a wall forming a 60° angle between the ground and the ladder. If the bottom of the ladder is 30 feet away from the wall, how long is the ladder?

A. $30\ feet$

B. $40\ feet$

C. $50\ feet$

D. $60\ feet$

19) If $x + y = 0$, $4x - 2y = 24$, which of the following ordered pairs (x, y) satisfies both equations?

A. $(4, 3)$

B. $(5, 4)$

C. $(4, -4)$

D. $(4, -6)$

20) If $f(x) = 3x + 4(x + 1) + 2$ then $f(3x) =?$

A. $21x + 6$

B. $16x - 6$

C. $25x + 4$

D. $12x + 3$

21) A line in the xy-plane passes through origin and has a slope of $\frac{2}{3}$. Which of the following points lies on the line?

A. $(2,1)$

B. $(4,1)$

C. $(9,6)$

D. $(9,3)$

22) In the figure below, what is the value of x?

A. 43

B. 83

C. 87

D. 90

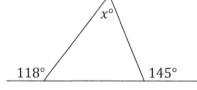

23) If $(ax + 4)(bx + 3) = 10x^2 + cx + 12$ for all values of x and $a + b = 7$, what are the two possible values for c?

A. $22, 21$

B. $20, 22$

C. $23, 26$

D. $24, 23$

24) Point A lies on the line with equation $y - 3 = 2(x + 5)$. If the x−coordinate of A is 8, what is the y−coordinate of A?

A. 14

B. 16

C. 22

D. 29

$$y < a - x \,,\, y > x + b$$

25) In the xy-plane, if $(0,0)$ is a solution to the system of inequalities above, which of the following relationships between a and b must be true?

A. $a < b$

B. $a > b$

C. $a = b$

D. $a = b + a$

STOP: This is the End of Section 2 of test 2.

ASVAB Mathematics Practice Test 2

2021

Section 1: Arithmetic Reasoning

Total number of questions: 30

Total time for this section 36 Minutes

You may NOT use a calculator on this Section.

1) Aria was hired to teach three identical math courses, which entailed being present in the classroom 36 hours altogether. At $25 per class hour, how much did Aria earn for teaching one course?

A. $50

B. $300

C. $600

D. $1,400

2) Karen is 9 years older than her sister Michelle, and Michelle is 4 years younger than her brother David. If the sum of their ages is 82, how old is Michelle?

A. 29

B. 27

C. 25

D. 23

3) John is driving to visit his mother, who lives 300 miles away. How long will the drive be, round−trip, if John drives at an average speed of 50 mph?

A. 95 *Minutes*

B. 260 *Minutes*

C. 645 *Minutes*

D. 720 *Minutes*

4) Julie gives 8 pieces of candy to each of her friends. If Julie gives all her candy away, which amount of candy could have been the amount she distributed?

A. 187

B. 216

C. 343

D. 223

5) There are only red and blue marbles in a box. The probability of choosing a red marble in the box at random is one fourth. If there are 132 blue marbles, how many marbles are in the box?

A. 140

B. 156

C. 176

D. 190

6) You are asked to chart the temperature during an 8 hour period to give the average. These are your results:

7 am: 2 degrees   11 am: 32 degrees

8 am: 5 degrees   12 pm: 35 degrees

9 am: 22 degrees   1 pm: 35 degrees

10 am: 28 degrees   2 pm: 33 degrees

What is the average temperature?

A. 36

B. 28

C. 24

D. 22

7) Each year, a cyber café charges its customers a base rate of $15, with an additional $0.20 per visit for the first 40 visits, and $0.10 for every visit after that. How much does the cyber café charge a customer for a year in which 60 visits are made?

A. $25

B. $29

C. $35

D. $39

8) If a vehicle is driven 32 miles on Monday, 35 miles on Tuesday, and 29 miles on Wednesday, what is the average number of miles driven each day?

A. 32 *Miles*

B. 31 *Miles*

C. 29 *Miles*

D. 27 *Miles*

9) Three co-workers contributed $10.25, $11.25, and $18.45 respectively to purchase a retirement gift for their boss. What is the maximum amount they can spend on a gift?

A. $42.25

B. $40.17

C. $39.95

D. $27.06

10) While at work, Emma checks her email once every 90 minutes. In 9–hour, how many times does she check her email?

A. 4 *Times*

B. 5 *Times*

C. 7 *Times*

D. 6 *Times*

11) A family owns 15 dozen of magazines. After donating 57 magazines to the public library, how many magazines are still with the family?

A. 180

B. 152

C. 123

D. 98

12) In the deck of cards, there are 4 spades, 3 hearts, 7 clubs, and 10 diamonds. What is the probability that William will pick out a spade?

A. $\frac{1}{6}$

B. $\frac{1}{8}$

C. $\frac{1}{9}$

D. $\frac{1}{5}$

13) What is the prime factorization of 560?

A. $2 \times 2 \times 5 \times 7$

B. $2 \times 2 \times 2 \times 2 \times 5 \times 7$

C. 2×7

D. $2 \times 2 \times 2 \times 5 \times 7$

14) William is driving a truck that can hold 5 tons maximum. He has a shipment of food weighing 32,000 pounds. How many trips will he need to make to deliver all of the food?

A. 1 *Trip*

B. 3 *Trips*

C. 4 *Trips*

D. 6 *Trips*

15) A man goes to a casino with $180. He loses $40 on blackjack, then loses another $50 on roulette. How much money does he have left?

A. $75

B. $90

C. $105

D. $120

16) A woman owns a dog walking business. If 3 workers can walk 9 dogs, how many dogs can 5 workers walk?

A. 13

B. 14

C. 15

D. 19

17) The mean of 50 test scores was calculated as 85. But, it turned out that one of the scores was misread as 94 but it was 69. What is the mean?

A. 84.5

B. 87

C. 87.5

D. 88.5

18) Mr. Carlos family are choosing a menu for their reception. They have 3 choices of appetizers, 7 choices of entrees, 4 choices of cake. How many different menu combinations are possible for them to choose?

A. 12

B. 32

C. 84

D. 120

19) Simplify the expression. $(5x^3 - 8x^2 + 2x^4) - (4x^2 - 2x^4 + 2x^3)$

A. $x^4 + 7x^3 - 8x^2$

B. $5x^4 + x^3 - 9x^2$

C. $4x^4 + 3x^3 - 12x^2$

D. $5x^4 + 2x^3 - 8x^2$

20) The average of five numbers is 24. If a sixth number 42 is added, then, what is the new average?

A. 25

B. 26

C. 27

D. 28

21)he ratio of two sides of a parallelogram is 2:3. If its perimeter is 40 *cm*, find the length of its sides.

A. 8 *cm*, 12 *cm*

B. 10 *cm*, 14 *cm*

C. 12 *cm*, 16 *cm*

D. 14 *cm*, 18 *cm*

22)88 students took an exam and 11 of them failed. What percent of the students passed the exam?

A. 20%

B. 40.3%

C. 60%

D. 87.5%

23)Removing which of the following numbers will change the average of the numbers to 6?

$$1, 4, 5, 8, 11, 12$$

A. 1

B. 4

C. 5

D. 11

24)In two successive years, the population of a town is increased by 12% and 25%. What percent of the population is increased after two years?

A. 34%

B. 38%

C. 40%

D. 60%

25) Five years ago, Amy was three times as old as Mike was. If Mike is 10 years old now, how old is Amy?

A. 4

B. 8

C. 12

D. 20

26) $(x^6)^{\frac{7}{8}}$ is equal to ...

A. $x^{\frac{19}{4}}$

B. $x^{\frac{21}{4}}$

C. $x^{\frac{23}{4}}$

D. $x^{\frac{25}{4}}$

27) A store has a container of handballs: 6 green, 5 blue, 8 white, and 10 yellow. If one ball is picked from the container at random, what is the probability that it will be green?

A. $\frac{1}{5}$

B. $\frac{6}{11}$

C. $\frac{6}{29}$

D. $\frac{8}{25}$

28) If 30% of a number is 12, what is the number?

A. 12

B. 25

C. 40

D. 45

29) If $x \blacksquare y = \sqrt{x^2 + y}$, what is the value of $6 \blacksquare 28$?

A. $\sqrt{168}$

B. 10

C. 8

D. 6

30) The Edwards School is ordering some tables. If x is the number of tables the school wants to order, which each costs \$100 and there is a one-time delivery charge of \$800, which of the following represents the total cost, in dollar, per table?

A. $100x + 800$

B. $100 + 800x$

C. $\frac{100x + 800}{100}$

D. $\frac{100x + 800}{x}$

STOP: This is the End of Section 1 of test 2.

ASVAB Mathematics Practice Test 2

2021

Section 2: Mathematics Knowledge

Total number of questions: 25

Total time for this section 24 Minutes

You may NOT use a calculator on this Section.

1) If $a = 3$, what is the value of b in this equation?

$$b = \frac{a^2}{3} + 3$$

A. 10

B. 8

C. 6

D. 4

2) The eighth root of 256 is:

A. 6

B. 4

C. 8

D. 2

3) A circle has a radius of 5 inches. What is its approximate area? ($\pi = 3.14$)

A. 90.7 *square inches*

B. 78.5 *square inches*

C. 31.4 *square inches*

D. 25 *square inches*

4) If $-8a = 64$, then $a = $ ___

A. -8

B. 8

C. 16

D. 0

5) In the following diagram what is the value of x?

A. 90°

B. 60°

C. 45°

D. 15°

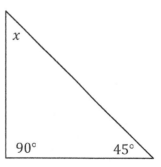

6) In the diagram below, circle A represents the set of all even numbers, circle B represents the set of all negative numbers, and circle C represents the set of all multiples of 6. Which number could be replaced with y?

A. 6

B. 0

C. −6

D. −10

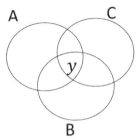

7) $(5x + 5)(2x + 6) = ?$

A. $5x + 6$

B. $10x^2 + 40x + 30$

C. $5x + 5x + 30$

D. $5x^2 + 5$

8) $5(a - 6) = 22$, what is the value of a?

A. 2.4

B. 10.4

C. 7

D. 11

9) If $3^{24} = 3^8 \times 3^x$, what is the value of x?

A. 2

B. 1.5

C. 3

D. 16

10) Which of the following is an obtuse angle?

A. 116°

B. 80°

C. 68°

D. 25°

11) Factor this expression: $x^2 + 5 - 6$

A. $x^2(5 + 6)$

B. $x(x + 5 - 6)$

C. $(x + 6)(x - 1)$

D. $(x + 6)(x - 6)$

12) Find the slope of the line running through the points $(6, 7)$ and $(5, 3)$.

A. $\frac{1}{4}$

B. $-\frac{1}{4}$

C. 4

D. -4

13) What is the value of $\sqrt{100} \times \sqrt{36}$?

A. 120

B. $\sqrt{136}$

C. 60

D. $\sqrt{16}$

14) Which of the following is not equal to 5^2?

A. the square of 5

B. 5 squared

C. 5 cubed

D. 5 to the second power

15) The cube root of 2,197 is?

A. 133

B. 13

C. 6.5

D. 169

16) What is 952,710 in scientific notation?

A. 95.271

B. 9.5271×10^5

C. 0.095271×10^6

D. 0.95271

17) What is the value of the expression $2(2x - y) + (4 - x)^2$ when $x = 2$ and $y = -1$?

A. -2

B. 8

C. 14

D. 28

18) A swimming pool holds 1,500 cubic feet of water. The swimming pool is 15 feet long and 10 feet wide. How deep is the swimming pool?

A. $2\ feet$

B. $4\ feet$

C. $6\ feet$

D. $10\ feet$

19) If $f(x) = x^3 - 2x^2 + 8x$ and $g(x) = 3$, what is the value of $f(g(x))$?

A. -3

B. 11

C. 22

D. 33

20) What is the solution of the following inequality?

$$|x - 2| \geq 4$$

A. $x \geq 6 \cup x \leq -2$

B. $-2 \leq x \leq 6$

C. $x \geq 6$

D. $x \leq -2$

21) Which of the following is equal to the expression below?

$$(3x - y)(2x + 2y)$$

A. $6x^2 - 2y^2$

B. $6x^2 + 4xy + 2y^2$

C. $12x^2 + 6xy + 2y^2$

D. $6x^2 + 4xy - 2y^2$

22) What is the product of all possible values of x in the following equation?

$$|x - 12| = 4$$

A. 4

B. 8

C. 16

D. 128

23) In the triangle below, if the measure of angle A is 37 degrees, then what is the value of y? (figure is NOT drawn to scale)

A. 62

B. 70

C. 78

D. 86

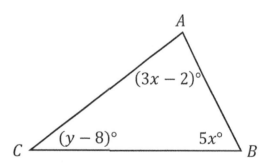

24) What is the perimeter of a square that has an area of 81 square inches?

A. 129 *inches*

B. 72 *inches*

C. 68 *inches*

D. 36 *inches*

25) What are the zeros of the function: $f(x) = x^2 - 7x + 12$?

A. 0

B. $-2, -3$

C. $0, 4, 3$

D. $4, 3$

STOP: This is the End of Section 2 of test 2.

ASVAB MATHEMATICS PRACTICE TESTS ANSWER KEYS

Now, it's time to review your results to see where you went wrong and what areas you need to improve.

ASVAB Math Practice Test 1							
Arithmetic Reasoning				Mathematics Knowledge			
1)	D	16)	D	1)	C	16)	C
2)	A	17)	A	2)	B	17)	B
3)	D	18)	B	3)	A	18)	D
4)	C	19)	C	4)	D	19)	C
5)	C	20)	D	5)	D	20)	A
6)	B	21)	C	6)	B	21)	C
7)	C	22)	C	7)	B	22)	B
8)	A	23)	C	8)	D	23)	C
9)	D	24)	A	9)	C	24)	D
10)	A	25)	C	10)	D	25)	B
11)	C	26)	C	11)	D		
12)	D	27)	D	12)	A		
13)	C	28)	C	13)	D		
14)	D	29)	C	14)	D		
15)	C	30)	C	15)	D		

ASVAB Math Practice Test 2							
Arithmetic Reasoning				**Mathematics Knowledge**			
1)	B	16)	C	1)	C	16)	B
2)	D	17)	A	2)	D	17)	C
3)	D	18)	C	3)	B	18)	D
4)	B	19)	C	4)	A	19)	D
5)	C	20)	C	5)	C	20)	A
6)	C	21)	A	6)	C	21)	D
7)	A	22)	D	7)	B	22)	D
8)	A	23)	D	8)	B	23)	D
9)	C	24)	C	9)	D	24)	D
10)	D	25)	D	10)	A	25)	D
11)	C	26)	B	11)	C		
12)	A	27)	C	12)	C		
13)	B	28)	C	13)	C		
14)	C	29)	C	14)	C		
15)	B	30)	C	15)	B		

ASVAB MATHEMATICS PRACTICE TESTS
ANSWERS AND EXPLANATIONS

ASVAB Practice Test 1: Arithmetic Reasoning

1) Choice D is correct

To compare fractions, find a common denominator. When two fractions have common denominators, the fraction with the larger numerator is the larger number. Choice A is incorrect because $\frac{3}{4}$ is not less than $\frac{17}{24}$. Write both fractions with common denominator and compare the numerators. $\frac{3}{4} = \frac{18}{24}$. The fraction $\frac{18}{24}$ is greater than $\frac{17}{24}$.

Choice B and C are not correct. Shown written with a common denominator, the comparisons $\frac{2}{3} < \frac{7}{9}$ and $\frac{3}{8} < \frac{9}{25}$ are not correct. Shown written with a common denominator, the comparison $\frac{11}{21} < \frac{4}{7}$ is correct because $\frac{4}{7}$ or $\frac{12}{21}$ is greater than $\frac{11}{21}$.

2) Choice A is correct

First multiply the tenths place of 7.8 by 4.56. The result is 3.648. Next, multiply 7 by 4.56 which results in 31.92. The sum of these two numbers is: $3.648 + 31.92 = 35.568$

3) Choice D is correct

Dividing 72 by 12%, which is equivalent to 0.12, gives 600. Therefore, 12% of 600 is 72.

4) Choice C is correct

$4 \div \frac{1}{3} = 12$

5) Choice C is correct

$\$8 \times 10 = \$80$, Petrol use: $10 \times 2 = 20$ liters
Petrol cost: $20 \times \$1 = \$20$. Money earned: $\$80 - \$20 = \$60$

6) Choice B is correct

$average \ (mean) = \frac{sum \ of \ terms}{number \ of \ terms} = \frac{7+11+14+16+19.5+16+14.5}{7} = 14$

7) Choice C is correct

Let x be the original price. If the price of the sofa is decreased by 20% to $476, then: $80\% \ of \ x = 476 \Rightarrow 0.80x = 476 \Rightarrow x = 476 \div 0.80 = 595$

8) Choice A is correct

The percent of girls playing tennis is: $45\% \times 25\% = 0.45 \times 0.25 = 0.11 = 11\%$

9) Choice D is correct

Write the equation and solve for B: $0.60A = 0.30B$, divide both sides by 0.30, then: $\frac{0.60}{0.30}A = B$, therefore: $B = 2A$, and B is 2 times of A or it's 200% of A.

10) Choice A is correct

Line AB is the best fit line. Then, point $(6,1)$ is the farthest from line AB.

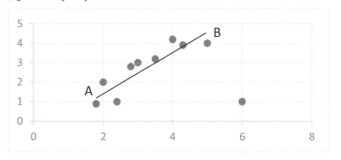

11) Choice C is correct

Th ratio of boy to girls is $4:7$. Therefore, there are 4 boys out of 11 students. To find the answer, first divide the total number of students by 11, then multiply the result by 4.
$55 \div 11 = 5 \Rightarrow 5 \times 4 = 20$. There are 20 boys and 35 $(55 - 20)$ girls. So, 15 more boys should be enrolled to make the ratio $1:1$

12) Choice D is correct

First simplify the multiplication: $\frac{5}{4} \times \frac{6}{2} = \frac{30}{8} = \frac{15}{4}$, Choice D is equal to $\frac{15}{4}$.
$\frac{5 \times 3}{4} = \frac{15}{4}$

13) Choice C is correct

Use percent formula: $part = \frac{prcent}{100} \times whole$
$35 = \frac{percent}{100} \times 20 \Rightarrow 35 = \frac{percent \times 20}{100} \Rightarrow 35 = \frac{percent \times 2}{10}$, multiply both sides by 10.
$350 = percent \times 2$, divide both sides by 2. $175 = percent$

14) Choice D is correct

Jason needs an 70% average to pass for five exams. Therefore, the sum of 5 exams must be at lease $5 \times 70 = 350$. The sum of 4 exams is: $68 + 72 + 85 + 90 = 315$. The minimum score Jason can earn on his fifth and final test to pass is: $350 - 315 = 35$

15) Choice C is correct

Use distance formula: $Distance = Rate \times time \Rightarrow 416 = 65 \times T$, divide both sides by 65. $416 \div 65 = T \Rightarrow T = 6.4 \ hours$.
Change hours to minutes for the decimal part. $0.4 \ hours = 0.4 \times 60 = 24 \ minutes$.

16) Choice D is correct

$average = \frac{sum \ of \ terms}{number \ of \ terms} \Rightarrow$ (average of 6 numbers) $14 = \frac{sum \ of \ numbers}{6} \Rightarrow$
sum of 6 numbers is $14 \times 6 = 84$, (average of 4 numbers) $10 = \frac{sum \ of \ numbers}{4} \Rightarrow$
sum of 4 numbers is $10 \times 4 = 40$.
$sum \ of \ 6 \ numbers - sum \ of \ 4 \ numbers = sum \ of \ 2 \ numbers$,
$84 - 40 = 44$ average of 2 numbers $= \frac{44}{2} = 22$

17) Choice A is correct

First, find the number. Let x be the number. Write the equation and solve for x.
150% of a number is 75, then: $1.5 \times x = 75 \Rightarrow x = 75 \div 1.5 = 50$, 80% of 50 is:
$0.8 \times 50 = 40$

18) Choice B is correct

$\frac{(8+6)^2}{2} + 6 = \frac{(14)^2}{2} + 6 = \frac{196}{2} + 6 = 98 + 6 = 104$

19) Choice C is correct

The weight of 14.2 meters of this rope is: $14.2 \times 600 \ g = 8,520 \ g$
$1 \ kg = 1,000 \ g$, therefore, $8,520 \ g \div 1,000 = 8.52 \ kg$

20) Choice D is correct

78 divided by 5, the remainder is 3. 45 divided by 7, the remainder is also 3.

21) Choice C is correct

Write a proportion and solve for x. $\frac{3}{2} = \frac{x}{26} \Rightarrow 2x = 3 \times 26 \Rightarrow x = 39 \ ft$

22) Choice C is correct

The distance between Jason and Joe is $9\ miles$. Jason running at $6.5\ miles\ per\ hour$ and Joe is running at the speed of $8\ miles\ per\ hour$. Therefore, every hour the distance is $1.5\ miles$ less.
$9 \div 1.5 = 6$

23) Choice C is correct

x is the number of all John's sales per month and 5% of it is: $5\% \times x = 0.05x$, John's monthly revenue: $0.05x + 4{,}500$

24) Choice A is correct

Plug in the value of x in the equation and solve for y. $2y = \frac{2x^2}{3} + 6 \rightarrow$
$2y = \frac{2(9)^2}{3} + 6 \rightarrow 2y = \frac{2(81)}{3} + 6 \rightarrow 2y = 54 + 6 = 60 \rightarrow 2y = 60 \rightarrow y = 30$

25) Choice C is correct

The average speed of john is: $150 \div 6 = 25$, The average speed of Alice is: $180 \div 4 = 45$
Write the ratio and simplify. $25:45 \Rightarrow 5:9$

26) Choice C is correct

Add the first 5 numbers. $40 + 45 + 50 + 35 + 55 = 225$
To find the distance traveled in the next 5 hours, multiply the average by number of hours.
$Distance = Average \times Rate = 50 \times 5 = 250$, Add both numbers. $250 + 225 = 475$

27) Choice D is correct

Th ratio of boy to girls is $2:3$. Therefore, there are 2 boys out of 5 students. To find the answer, first divide the total number of students by 5, then multiply the result by 2.
$600 \div 5 = 120 \Rightarrow 120 \times 2 = 240$

28) Choice C is correct

Use percent formula: $part = \frac{percent}{100} \times whole$

$25 = \frac{percent}{100} \times 20 \Rightarrow 25 = \frac{percent \times 20}{100} \Rightarrow 25 = \frac{percent \times 2}{10}$, multiply both sides by 10.

$250 = percent \times 2$, divide both sides by 2. $125 = percent$

29) Choice C is correct

Let x be the number. Write the equation and solve for x.

$\frac{2}{3} \times 18 = \frac{2}{5} . x \Rightarrow \frac{2 \times 18}{3} = \frac{2x}{5}$, use cross multiplication to solve for x.

$5 \times 36 = 2x \times 3 \Rightarrow 180 = 6x \Rightarrow x = 30$

30) Choice C is correct

The question is this: 1.75 is what percent of 1.25? Use percent formula:

$$part = \frac{percent}{100} \times whole$$

$1.75 = \frac{percent}{100} \times 1.25 \Rightarrow 1.75 = \frac{percent \times 1.25}{100} \Rightarrow 175 = percent \times 1.25 \Rightarrow$

$percent = \frac{175}{1.25} = 140$

ASVAB PRACTICE TEST 1: MATHEMATICS KNOWLEDGE

1) Choice C is correct

Let x be the number. Write the equation and solve for x. $(24 - x) \div x = 3$. Multiply both sides by x. $(24 - x) = 3x$, then add x both sides. $24 = 4x$, now divide both sides by 4. $x = 6$

2) Choice B is correct

The sum of supplement angles is 180. Let x be that angle. Therefore, $x + 5x = 180$
$6x = 180$, divide both sides by 6: $x = 30$

3) Choice A is correct

The sum of all angles in a quadrilateral is 360 degrees. Let x be the smallest angle in the quadrilateral. Then the angles are: $x, 2x, 3x, 4x$,
$x + 2x + 3x + 4x = 360 \to 10x = 360 \to x = 36$, The angles in the quadrilateral are: $36°, 72°, 108°$, and $144°$, The smallest angle is 36 degrees.

4) Choice D is correct

Use Pythagorean Theorem: $a^2 + b^2 = c^2$, $6^2 + 8^2 = c^2 \Rightarrow 100 = c^2 \Rightarrow c = 10$

5) Choice D is correct

The perimeter of the trapezoid is 54.
Therefore, the missing side (height) is $= 54 - 18 - 12 - 14 = 10$
Area of the trapezoid: $A = \frac{1}{2}h(b_1 + b_2) = \frac{1}{2}(10)(12 + 14) = 130$

6) Choice B is correct

Use the formula of areas of circles. $Area = \pi r^2 \Rightarrow 25\pi = \pi r^2 \Rightarrow 25 = r^2 \Rightarrow r = 5$
Radius of the circle is 5. Now, use the circumference formula:
Circumference $= 2\pi r = 2\pi(5) = 10\pi$

7) Choice B is correct

Use the information provided in the question to draw the shape.
Use Pythagorean Theorem: $a^2 + b^2 = c^2$
$40^2 + 30^2 = c^2 \Rightarrow 1,600 + 900 = c^2 \Rightarrow 2,500 = c^2 \Rightarrow c = 50$

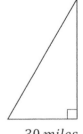

40 miles

30 miles

8) Choice D is correct

Surface Area of a cylinder $= 2\pi r(r+h)$, The radius of the cylinder is 8 inches and its height is 12 inches. Surface Area of a cylinder $= 2(\pi)(8)(8+12) = 320\pi$

9) Choice C is correct

Use simple interest formula:
$I = prt$, (I = interest, p = principal, r = rate, t = time)
$I = (8,000)(0.045)(5) = 1,800$

10) Choice D is correct

$(4.2 \times 10^6) \times (2.6 \times 10^{-5}) = (4.2 \times 2.6) \times (10^6 \times 10^{-5}) = 10.92 \times (10^{6+(-5)}) = 1.092 \times 10^2$

11) Choice D is correct

The formula of the volume of pyramid is: $V = \frac{l \times w \times h}{3}$. The length and width of the pyramid is $6\ cm$ and its height is $12\ cm$. Therefore: $V = \frac{6 \times 6 \times 12}{3} = 144\ cm^3$

12) Choice A is correct

$|-13 - 6| - |-9 + 3| = |-19| - |-6| = 19 - 6 = 13$

13) Choice D is correct

Use distributive property: $2x(4 + 2y) = 8x + 4xy = 4xy + 8x$

14) Choice D is correct

$y = 4ab + 3b^3$, plug in the values of a and b in the equation: $a = 2$ and $b = 3$,
$y = 4ab + 3b^3 \rightarrow y = 4(2)(3) + 3(3^3) = 24 + 81 = 105$

15) Choice D is correct

Solve for x. $-2 \leq 2x - 4 < 8 \Rightarrow$ (add 4 all sides) $-2 + 4 \leq 2x - 4 + 4 < 8 + 4 \Rightarrow$
$2 \leq 2x < 12 \Rightarrow$ (divide all sides by 2) $1 \leq x < 6$
x is between 1 and 6. Choice D represent this inequality.

16) Choice C is correct

Set of number that are not composite between 1 and 25:
$A = \{1, 2, 3, 5, 7, 11, 13, 17, 19, 23\}$

$$Probability = \frac{number\ of\ desired\ outcomes}{number\ of\ total\ outcomes} = \frac{10}{25} = \frac{2}{5}$$

17) Choice B is correct

Plug in each pair of number in the equation:
A. $(2,1)$: $2(2) + 4(1) = 8$
B. $(-1,3)$: $2(-1) + 4(3) = 10$
C. $(-2,2)$: $2(-2) + 4(2) = 4$
D. $(2,2)$: $2(2) + 4(2) = 12$
Only Choice B is correct.

18) Choice D is correct

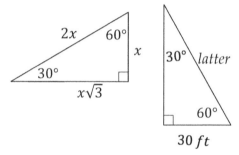

The relationship among all sides
of special right triangle
$30° - 60° - 90°$ is provided in this triangle:
In this triangle, the opposite side
of $30°$ angle is half of the hypotenuse.
Draw the shape of this question:
The latter is the hypotenuse. Therefore, the latter is $60\ ft$

19) Choice C is correct

Method 1: Plugin the values of x and y provided in the options into both equations.
A. $(4,3)$ $x + y = 0 \rightarrow 4 + 3 \neq 0$
B. $(5,4)$ $x + y = 0 \rightarrow 5 + 4 \neq 0$
C. $(4,-4)$ $x + y = 0 \rightarrow 4 + (-4) = 0$
D. $(4,-6)$ $x + y = 0 \rightarrow 4 + (-6) \neq 0$
Only option C is correct.
Method 2: Multiplying each side of $x + y = 0$ by 2 gives $2x + 2y = 0$. Then, adding the corresponding side of $2x + 2y = 0$ and $4x - 2y = 24$ gives $6x = 24$. Dividing each side of $6x = 24$ by 6 gives $x = 4$. Finally, substituting 4 for x in $x + y = 0$, or $y = -4$. Therefore, the solution to the given system of equations is $(4,-4)$.

20) Choice A is correct

If $f(x) = 3x + 4(x + 1) + 2$, then find $f(3x)$ by substituting $3x$ for every x in the function. This gives: $f(3x) = 3(3x) + 4(3x + 1) + 2$
It simplifies to: $f(3x) = 3(3x) + 4(3x + 1) + 2 = 9x + 12x + 4 + 2 = 21x + 6$

21) Choice C is correct

First, find the equation of the line. All lines through the origin are of the form $y = mx$, so the equation is $y = \frac{2}{3}x$. Of the given choices, only choice C (9,6), satisfies this equation:
$$y = \frac{2}{3}x \rightarrow 6 = \frac{2}{3}(9) = 6$$

22) Choice B is correct

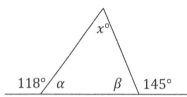

Let's find the angles α and β.
$\alpha = 180° - 118° = 62°$
$\beta = 180° - 145° = 35°$
All angles in a triangle sum up to 180 degrees. Then:
$x + \alpha + \beta = 180° \rightarrow x = 180° - 62° - 35° = 83°$

23) Choice C is correct

You can find the possible values of a and b in $(ax + 4)(bx + 3)$ by using the given equation $a + b = 7$ and finding another equation that relates the variables a and b. Since $(ax + 4)(bx + 3) = 10x^2 + x + 12$, expand the left side of the equation to obtain
$abx^2 + 4bx + 3ax + 12 = 10x^2 + cx + 12$
Since ab is the coefficient of x^2 on the left side of the equation and 10 is the coefficient of x^2 on the right side of the equation, it must be true that $ab = 10$
The coefficient of x on the left side is $4b + 3a$ and the coefficient of x in the right side is c. Then: $4b + 3a = c, \quad a + b = 7$, then: $a = 7 - b$
Now, plug in the value of a in the equation $ab = 10$. Then:
$ab = 10 \rightarrow (7 - b)b = 10 \rightarrow 7b - b^2 = 10$
Add $-7b + b^2$ both sides. Then: $b^2 - 7b + 10 = 0$
Solve for b using the factoring method. $b^2 - 7b + 10 = 0 \rightarrow (b - 5)(b - 2) = 0$
Thus, either $b = 2$ and $a = 5$, or $b = 5$ and $a = 2$. If $b = 2$ and $a = 5$, then $4b + 3a = c \rightarrow 4(2) + 3(5) = c \rightarrow c = 23$. If $5 = 2$ and $a = 2$, then, $4b + 3a = c \rightarrow 4(5) + 3(2) = c \rightarrow c = 26$. Therefore, the two possible values for c are 23 and 26.

24) Choice D is correct

Here we can substitute 8 for x in the equation. Thus, $y - 3 = 2(8 + 5), y - 3 = 26$
Adding 3 to both side of the equation: $y = 26 + 3, \qquad y = 29$

25) Choice B is correct

Since $(0, 0)$ is a solution to the system of inequalities, substituting 0 for x and 0 for y in the given system must result in two true inequalities. After this substitution, $y < a - x$ becomes $0 < a$, and $y > x + b$ becomes $0 > b$. Hence, a is positive and b is negative. Therefore, $a > b$.

ASVAB PRACTICE TEST 2: ARITHMETIC REASONING

1) Choice B is correct

$36 \div 3 = 12$ hours for one course, $12 \times 25 = 300 \Rightarrow \$300$

2) Choice D is correct

Karen = Michelle + 9, Michelle = David − 4,
Michelle = David − 4 → David = Michele +4, Karen + Michelle + David = 82
Now, replace the ages of Karen and David by Michelle.
Then: Michelle + 9 + Michelle + Michelle + 4 = 82, 3Michelle + 13 = 82
$\Rightarrow$ 3Michelle = 82 − 13; 3Michelle = 69, $\Rightarrow$ Michelle = 23

3) Choice D is correct

$$distance = speed \times time \Rightarrow time = \frac{distance}{speed} = \frac{600}{50} = 12$$

(Round trip means that the distance is 600 miles)

The round trip takes 12 hours. Change hours to minutes, then: $12 \times 60 = 720$

4) Choice B is correct

Since Julie gives 8 pieces of candy to each of her friends, then, then number of pieces of candies must be divisible by 8.

A. $187 \div 8 = 23.375$

B. $216 \div 8 = 27$

C. $343 \div 8 = 42.875$

D. $223 \div 8 = 27.875$

Only choice B gives a whole number.

5) Choice C is correct

let x be total number of marbles in the box, then number of red marbles is: $x - 132$

$p = \frac{1}{4} = \frac{x-132}{x}$, Use cross multiplication to solve for x.

$x = 4(x - 132) \to x = 4x - 528 \to 3x = 528 \to x = 176$

6) Choice C is correct

$average = \frac{sum}{total}$, $Sum = 2 + 5 + 22 + 28 + 32 + 35 + 35 + 33 = 192$

Total number of numbers $= 8$, $average = \frac{192}{8} = 24$

7) Choice A is correct

The base rate is \$15. The fee for the first 40 visits is: $40 \times 0.20 = 8$

The fee for the visits 41 to 60 is: $20 \times 0.10 = 2$, Total charge: $15 + 8 + 2 = 25$

8) Choice A is correct

$average = \frac{sum}{total} = \frac{32+35+29}{3} = \frac{96}{3} = 32$

9) Choice C is correct

The amount they have $= \$10.25 + \$11.25 + \$18.45 = 39.95$

10) Choice D is correct

Change 9 hours to minutes, then: $9 \times 60 = 540 \; minutes$, $\frac{540}{90} = 6$

11) Choice C is correct

15 dozen of magazines are 180 magazines: $15 \times 12 = 180$, $\quad 180 - 57 = 123$

12) Choice A is correct

$probability = \frac{desired\ outcomes}{possible\ outcomes} = \frac{4}{4+3+7+10} = \frac{4}{24} = \frac{1}{6}$

13) Choice B is correct

Find the value of each choice:

A. $2 \times 2 \times 5 \times 7 = 140$

B. $2 \times 2 \times 2 \times 2 \times 5 \times 7 = 560$

C. $2 \times 7 = 14$

D. $2 \times 2 \times 2 \times 5 \times 7 = 280$

14) Choice C is correct

1 ton = 2,000 pounds, 5 ton = 10,000 pounds, $\frac{32,000}{10,000} = 3.2$

William needs to make at least 4 trips to deliver all of the food.

15) Choice B is correct

$180 - 40 - 50 = 90$

16) Choice C is correct

Each worker can walk 3 dogs: $9 \div 3 = 3$, 5 workers can walk 15 dogs. $5 \times 3 = 15$

17) Choice A is correct

$$average\ (mean) = \frac{sum\ of\ terms}{number\ of\ terms} \Rightarrow 85 = \frac{sum\ of\ terms}{50} \Rightarrow sum = 85 \times 50 = 4,250$$

The difference of 94 and 69 is 25. Therefore, 25 should be subtracted from the sum.

$$4250 - 25 = 4,225, \quad mean = \frac{sum\ of\ terms}{number\ of\ terms} \Rightarrow mean = \frac{4,225}{50} = 84.5$$

18) Choice C is correct

To find the number of possible outfit combinations, multiply number of options for each factor: $3 \times 7 \times 4 = 84$

19) Choice C is correct

Simplify and combine like terms.
$(5x^3 - 8x^2 + 2x^4) - (4x^2 - 2x^4 + 2x^3) \Rightarrow 5x^3 - 8x^2 + 2x^4 - 4x^2 + 2x^4 - 2x^3 \Rightarrow$
$4x^4 + 3x^3 - 12x^2$

20) Choice C is correct

Solve for the sum of five numbers.

$$average = \frac{sum\ of\ terms}{number\ of\ terms} \Rightarrow 24 = \frac{sum\ of\ 5\ numbers}{5} \Rightarrow$$

$sum\ of\ 5\ numbers = 24 \times 5 = 120$

The sum of 5 numbers is 120. If a sixth number 42 is added, then the sum of 6 numbers is

$120 + 42 = 162, \ average = \dfrac{sum \ of \ terms}{number \ of \ terms} = \dfrac{162}{6} = 27$

21) Choice A is correct

Let the lengths of two sides of the parallelogram be $2x \ cm$ and $3x \ cm$ respectively.
Then, its perimeter $= 2(2x + 3x) = 10x$
Therefore, $10x = 40 \rightarrow x = 4$
One side $= 2(4) = 8 \ cm$ and other side is: $3(4) = 12 \ cm$

22) Choice D is correct

The failing rate is 11 out of $88 = \dfrac{11}{88}$, Change the fraction to percent:

$\dfrac{11}{88} \times 100\% = 12.5\%$

12.5 percent of students failed. Therefore, 87.5 percent of students passed the exam.

23) Choice D is correct

Check each choice provided:

A. 1 $\dfrac{4+5+8+11+12}{5} = \dfrac{40}{5} = 8$

B. 4 $\dfrac{1+5+8+11+12}{5} = \dfrac{37}{5} = 7.4$

C. 5 $\dfrac{1+4+8+11+12}{5} = \dfrac{36}{5} = 7.2$

D. 11 $\dfrac{1+4+5+8+12}{5} = \dfrac{30}{5} = 6$

24) Choice C is correct

The population is increased by 12% and 25%. 12% increase changes the population to 112% of original population. For the second increase, multiply the result by 125%: $(1.12) \times (1.25) = 1.40 = 140\%$, 40 percent of the population is increased after two years.

25) Choice D is correct

Five years ago, Amy was three times as old as Mike. Mike is 10 years now. Therefore, 5 years ago Mike was 5 years. Five years ago, Amy was: $A = 3 \times 5 = 15$, Now Amy is 20 years old: $15 + 5 = 20$

26) Choice B is correct

Multiply two exponents: $(x^6)^{\frac{7}{8}} = x^{6 \times \frac{7}{8}} = x^{\frac{42}{8}} = x^{\frac{21}{4}}$

27) Choice C is correct

The total number of handballs in the container is $6 + 5 + 8 + 10 = 29$. Since there are 6 green handballs, the probability of selecting a green handball is $\frac{6}{29}$.

28) Choice C is correct

Let x be the number. Write the equation and solve for x.

30% of $x = 12 \Rightarrow 0.30x = 12 \Rightarrow x = 12 \div 0.30 = 40$

29) Choice C is correct

Substitute x by 6 and y by 28 in the equation. Then:

$6 \blacksquare 28 = \sqrt{6^2 + 28} = \sqrt{36 + 28} = \sqrt{64} = 8$

30) Choice C is correct

The amount of money for x tables is: $100x$, then, the total cost of all tables is equal to: $100x + 800$, the total cost, in dollar, per table is: $\frac{Total\ cost}{number\ of\ tables} = \frac{100x + 800}{x}$

ASVAB PRACTICE TEST 2: MATHEMATICS KNOWLEDGE

1) **Choice C is correct**

   If $a = 3$ then: $b = \frac{a^2}{3} + 3 \Rightarrow b = \frac{3^2}{3} + 3 = 3 + 3 = 6$

2) **Choice D is correct**

   $\sqrt[8]{256} = 2$, $(2^8 = 2 \times 2 \times 2 \times 2 \times 2 \times 2 \times 2 \times 2 = 256)$

3) **Choice B is correct**

   (r = radius) Area of a circle $= \pi r^2 = \pi \times (5)^2 = 3.14 \times 25 = 78.5$

4) **Choice A is correct**

   $-8a = 64 \Rightarrow a = \frac{64}{-8} = -8$

5) **Choice C is correct**

   All angles in a triable add up to 180 degrees.
   $90° + 45° = 135°, x = 180° - 135° = 45°$

6) **Choice C is correct**

   y is the intersection of the three circles. Therefore, it must be even (from circle A), negative (from circle B), and multiple of 6 (from circle C). From the choice, only -6 is even, negative and multiple of 6.

7) **Choice B is correct**

   Use FOIL (first, out, in, last) method.
   $(5x + 5)(2x + 6) = 10x^2 + 30x + 10x + 30 = 10x^2 + 40x + 30$

8) **Choice B is correct**

   $5(a - 6) = 22 \Rightarrow 5a - 30 = 22 \Rightarrow 5a = 22 + 30 \Rightarrow 5a = 52 \Rightarrow a = \frac{52}{5} = 10.4$

9) **Choice D is correct**

   Use exponent multiplication rule: $x^a . x^b = x^{a+b}$ Then: $3^{24} = 3^8 \times 3^x = 3^{8+x}$
   $24 = 8 + x \Rightarrow x = 24 - 8 \Rightarrow x = 16$

10) Choice A is correct

An obtuse angle is an angle of greater than 90 degrees and less than 180 degrees. Only choice A is an obtuse angle.

11) Choice C is correct

To factor the expression $x^2 + 5 - 6$, we need to find two numbers whose sum is 5 and their product is -6. Those numbers are 6 and -1. Then:
$x^2 + 5 - 6 = (x + 6)(x - 1)$

12) Choice C is correct

Slope of a line: $\frac{y_2 - y_1}{x_2 - x_1} = \frac{rise}{run} \rightarrow \frac{y_2 - y_1}{x_2 - x_1} = \frac{3-7}{5-6} = \frac{-4}{-1} = 4$

13) Choice C is correct

$\sqrt{100} = 10$, $\sqrt{36} = 6$, $10 \times 6 = 60$

14) Choice C is correct

Only choice C is not equal to 5^2.

15) Choice B is correct

$\sqrt[3]{2,197} = 13$

16) Choice B is correct

In scientific notation form, numbers are written with one whole number times 10 to the power of a whole number. Number 952,710 has 6 digits. Write the number and after the first digit put the decimal point. Then, multiply the number by 10 to the power of 5 (number of remaining digits).
Then: $952,710 = 9.5271 \times 10^5$

17) Choice C is correct

Plug in the value of x and y: $x = 2$ and $y = -1$
$2(2x - y) + (4 - x)^2 = 2(2(2) - (-1)) + (4 - 2)^2 = 2(4 + 1) + (2)^2 = 10 + 4 = 14$

18) Choice D is correct

Use formula of rectangle prism volume: $V = (length)(width)(height) \Rightarrow$
$1,500 = (15)(10)(height) \Rightarrow height = 1,500 \div 150 = 10$

19) Choice D is correct

$g(x) = 3$, then $f(g(x)) = f(3) = (3)^3 - 2(3)^2 + 8(3) = 27 - 18 + 24 = 33$

20) Choice A is correct

$|x - 2| \geq 4$. Then: $x - 2 \geq 4$ or $x - 2 \leq 4$. Solve both inequalities:
$x - 2 \geq 4 \rightarrow x \geq 6$ and $x - 2 \leq -4 \rightarrow x \leq -2$.
The solution of the inequality $|x - 2| \geq 4$ is $x \geq 6 \cup x \leq -2$

21) Choice D is correct

Use FOIL method: $(3x - y)(2x + 2y) = 6x^2 + 6xy - 2xy - 2y^2 = 6x^2 + 4xy - 2y^2$

22) Choice D is correct

To solve absolute values equations, write two equations. $x - 12$ could be positive 4, or negative -4. Therefore, $x - 12 = 4 \Rightarrow x = 16$, $x - 12 = -4 \Rightarrow x = 8$. Find the product of solutions: $8 \times 16 = 128$

23) Choice D is correct

In the figure angle A is labeled $(3x - 2)$ and it measures 37. Thus, $3x - 2 = 37$ and $3x = 39$ or $x = 13$. That means that angle B, which is labeled $(5x)$, must measure $5 \times 13 = 65$.
Since the three angles of a triangle must add up to 180, $37 + 65 + y - 8 = 180$, then: $y + 94 = 108 \rightarrow y = 180 - 94 = 86$

24) Choice D is correct

The area of the square is 81 inches. Therefore, the side of the square is square root of the area. $\sqrt{81} = 9$ inches. Four times the side of the square is the perimeter: $4 \times 9 = 36\ inches$

25) Choice D is correct

First factor the function: $(x - 4)(x - 3)$. To find the zeros, $f(x)$ should be zero: $f(x) = (x - 4)(x - 3) = 0$, Therefore, the zeros are, $(x - 4) = 0 \Rightarrow x = 4$, $(x - 3) = 0 \Rightarrow x = 3$

www.EffortlessMath.com

... So Much More Online!

- ❖ FREE Math lessons

- ❖ More Math learning books!

- ❖ Mathematics Worksheets

- ❖ Online Math Tutors

Need a PDF version of this book?

Visit www.EffortlessMath.com

Receive the PDF version of this book or get another FREE book!

Thank you for using our Book!

Do you LOVE this book?

Then, you can get the PDF version of this book or another book absolutely FREE!

Please email us at:

info@EffortlessMath.com

for details.

Author's Final Note

I hope you enjoyed reading this book. You've made it through the book! Great job!

First of all, thank you for purchasing this study guide. I know you could have picked any number of books to help you prepare for your GED Math test, but you picked this book and for that I am extremely grateful.

It took me years to write this study guide for the GED Math because I wanted to prepare a comprehensive GED Math study guide to help test takers make the most effective use of their valuable time while preparing for the test.

After teaching and tutoring GED math for over a decade, I've gathered my personal notes and lessons to develop this study guide. It is my greatest hope that the lessons in this book could help you prepare for your test successfully.

If you have any questions, please contact me at reza@effortlessmath.com and I will be glad to assist. Your feedback will help me to greatly improve the quality of my books in the future and make this book even better. Furthermore, I expect that I have made a few minor errors somewhere in this study guide. If you think this to be the case, please let me know so I can fix the issue as soon as possible.

If you enjoyed this book and found some benefit in reading this, I'd like to hear from you and hope that you could take a quick minute to post a review on the book's Amazon page. To leave your valuable feedback, please visit: amzn.to/34Ngvrn

Or scan this QR code.

I personally go over every single review, to make sure my books really are reaching out and helping students and test takers. Please help me help GED Math test takers, by leaving a review!

I wish you all the best in your future success!

Reza Nazari

Math teacher and author

Made in the USA
Coppell, TX
30 August 2021

61444468R00116